ENTERTAINING

Fast & Fresh

by SUSAN MITCHELL

Ideals Publishing Corp.
Nashville, Tennessee

Director of Publishing: Patricia Pingry
Managing Editor: Marybeth Owens
Cookbook Editor: Cornell M. Brellenthin
Photographer: Gerald Koser
Food Stylist: Lisa Landers
Typographer: Kim Kaczanowski
Copy Editors: Linda Robinson, Shelly Bowerman

Published by
Ideals Publishing Corporation
Nelson Place, Elm Hill Pike
Nashville, Tennessee
Printed simultaneously in Canada.

Cover Recipes:
Lamb Chops Persillade, Rice Pilaf with Vegetables, and
Tomato Shells with Vegetable Purée, page 10.

Photograph of Susan Mitchell
by J. Edward Ouellette,
Los Angeles, California.

CONTENTS

INTRODUCTION
by
SUSAN MITCHELL

Most of us prefer to visit with guests around an attractive dinner table, rather than through a swinging kitchen door. Keeping this in mind, I have streamlined classic recipes into contemporary delights. This process has evolved from a combination of nutritional training in home economics at Washington State University and artistic acquisitions from the London Cordon Bleu School of Cooking. This education, along with practical and busy, day-to-day living, has directed me toward a food philosophy embracing fresh ingredients, speedily prepared and aesthetically presented. The result is a healthy and elegant dining experience.

Entertaining Fast and Fresh is comprised of planned menus for four, and can be your simple secret to successful entertaining. Recipes are designed to eliminate time-consuming traditional procedures that involve unnecessary steps and an excess of pots and pans. Each menu offers a variety of color, texture, and flavor.

Keep these creative concepts in mind as you mix and match menus to reflect your own personality. Sometimes you'll find it easier to serve foods "family style;" at other times, pre-plating and perhaps pooling a sauce *under* an entrée results in a prettier presentation. Utilize raw, whole foods from component ingredients in a sauce or dish to garnish a meal. Unusual ingredients, bright colors, and surprising shapes all serve to catch the eye. Simply garnishing an entrée with a sprig of the fresh herb used in its preparation is a nice touch. Fragrant herbs, in miniature planters, also make quaint centerpieces for a rustic dining atmosphere.

The way you arrange your table is as much a reflection of your individual style as is the food you like to serve. Your choice of theme, color, candles, cloths, mats, and table service introduces the mood. Bright ribbons, runners, bows, and flowers provide additional accents.

Basil Shrimp and Zucchini Appetizer, page 93.

Flowers should be decorative without being obtrusive; keep in mind the size of your table and everything else that has to go on it. For a formal dining table, incorporate small, individual flower arrangements adjacent to each place setting. Do not feel you must always have fresh flowers; silk or dried are equally effective alternatives. They also enable you to avoid searching for blooms that may not be in season, and you don't have to worry about an overscented bouquet that may compete with the aroma of your fine food.

If you decide to use candles, keep them unscented, also. Select non-drip varieties and make sure they are firmly fixed. Dim your household lights and arrange candles so that the immediate dining area is bathed in soft light; company should have enough light to see your colorful cooking. Candles should not obstruct freedom of movement or the ability to see one another; this could hinder the flow of pleasant conversation.

Conversation may center around intriguing accents you use to enhance an international setting. Float blossoms in finger bowls and fold napkins into fans for an Oriental aura. An arrangement of votive candles, sea shells, and conches lends a Mediterranean atmosphere to a seafood menu. Try hanging a colorful pinata *securely* over the dining table to carry out a festive Mexican theme. Don't hesitate to be creative, guests will appreciate your novelty.

Remember, entertaining is for your enjoyment, too. It can be a leisurely and lovely experience for you and your guests. Omitting exhausting hours in the kitchen, this cookbook frees you for creative indulgence. Behind *Entertaining Fast and Fresh*, is my belief that nothing lends itself more to successful entertaining than your presence.

> Chicken Liver Paté with Armagnac
> Lamb Chops Persillade
> Rice Pilaf with Vegetables
> Tomato Shells with Vegetable Purée

*Bright red tomatoes filled with green vegetable purée bring
color and drama to an elegant menu. Create your own
variation by substituting other colorful vegetables for the purée.
Vary the seasonings, too! Enjoy the vegetables in the rice,
also; they are cooked only by the heat of the rice,
retaining vitamins, crispness, and flavor.*

Chicken Liver Paté with Armagnac
Makes 4 servings

¼ cup butter
1 pound chicken livers, halved
¼ pound mushrooms, chopped
¼ cup chopped parsley
¼ cup chopped shallots
½ teaspoon thyme leaves
½ teaspoon basil leaves
2 to 3 tablespoons Armagnac, Cognac,
  or Madeira

½ cup dry red wine
1 cup butter
1 can (³⁄₇ ounce) black truffles
  or ¼ cup chopped pistachios *or*
  3 tablespoons green peppercorns,
  optional

Melt butter over medium-high heat in a wide frying pan. Add next 6 ingredients and sauté, stirring often, until livers are just firm but slightly pink in center. In small frying pan, warm Armagnac and flambe. Add to livers and shake until flame dies. Add wine, heat to simmering; then let mixture cool to room temperature. Process or blend entire mixture. Add butter in chunks, blending until smooth. Fold in truffles, if desired. Pour mixture into a deep 4 to 5-cup loaf pan. Cover and chill overnight. Serve with paté knife.

Note: Paté can be prepared up to one week in advance. Cover and refrigerate until serving time.

Lamb Chops Persillade

Makes 4 servings

4 lamb loin chops, cut ¾ to 1 inch thick
2 cloves garlic, minced and stirred to a paste
1 tablespoon butter
3 tablespoons finely minced shallots *or* green onion

⅓ cup fine bread crumbs
⅓ cup minced fresh parsley
1 teaspoon tarragon, basil, *or* thyme
Freshly ground pepper
Grated Parmesan cheese

Line the broiler pan with foil to collect drippings. Rub chops with garlic paste. Broil 4 inches from heat source for 6 to 8 minutes on each side. Melt butter in a saucepan; sauté shallots and bread crumbs until golden brown. Remove from heat. Stir in parsley, herbs, and drippings from lamb chops. Add pepper and cheese to taste. Spread over one side of chops just before serving.

Rice Pilaf with Vegetables

Makes 4 servings

3 cups chicken broth
1 cup wild and white rice mixture *or* brown rice
1 small red onion, finely chopped

5 or 6 mushrooms, finely chopped
1 stalk celery, finely chopped
3 tablespoons minced fresh parsley

Bring the broth to a boil. Stir in rice and simmer, covered, until rice is cooked and liquid is absorbed. Stir vegetables and parsley into hot rice.

Variations

◆ **Pimiento Pilaf:** Stir in chopped pimiento, cilantro, *or* watercress.
◆ **Herb Pilaf:** Stir in ½ bay leaf, crumbled, and ½ teaspoon herb of your choice.
◆ **Nutty Pilaf:** Stir in toasted pine nuts *or* almonds.

Tomato Shells with Vegetable Purée

Makes 4 servings

1 pound broccoli, coarsely chopped
2 chayotes, peeled and sliced
2 large tomatoes, at room temperature
¼ cup Neufchatel cheese

¼ cup ricotta cheese
Dash nutmeg *or* cayenne
Freshly ground pepper
Grated Romano cheese

Steam broccoli and chayote until tender, about 12 minutes. Make deep zigzag cuts around the circumference of the tomatoes; twist and pull gently to separate into halves. Scoop out pulp and seeds; set tomato shells aside on a warm platter. In a blender or food processor, process green vegetables, Neufchatel, ricotta, nutmeg, and pepper until mixture is smooth. Pour hot purée into tomato shells. Sprinkle with Romano cheese. Broil until cheese is golden and tomato is hot.

Tomato Shells with Vegetable Purée, Lamb Chops Persillade and Rice Pilaf with Vegetables, this page.

Chicken Puffs
Trout Meuniere
Fresh Asparagus with Blender Bearnaise
Squash and Mushrooms with Herbs
Spinach Salad with
Lemon-Lime Vinaigrette

This menu demonstrates how vegetables can provide color, taste, and nutrition, without starchy calories. A hearty Blender Bearnaise recipe is included; however, asparagus is also delicious and simple, when served with the excess Trout Meuniere Sauce.

Chicken Puffs

Makes 1 dozen pastries

½ package (10 ounces) puff pastry sheets
1 tablespoon butter
1 small red onion, minced
2 teaspoons curry
1 teaspoon chopped chutney

1 tablespoon chopped walnuts *or* almonds
1 tablespoon shredded coconut
½ cup half-and-half
1 cup chopped cooked chicken

Roll out one sheet puff pastry. Cut out 1½-inch rounds with fluted cookie cutter. Bake in oven according to package directions. Melt butter in a large saucepan. Sauté onion until golden. Stir in curry, chutney, nuts, and coconut; cook 3 to 5 minutes. Add half-and-half and bring to a boil. Simmer 5 minutes. Add chicken and blend well. Serve warm or cold on puff pastry shells.

Squash and Mushrooms with Herbs

Makes 4 servings

1 pound (4 small) crookneck *or* zucchini squash, quartered
½ pound mushrooms, halved

¼ cup chicken broth
½ teaspoon dried basil *or* tarragon
Salt and freshly ground pepper

Place all ingredients in a skillet; cover and simmer until tender-crisp, 6 to 8 minutes.

Trout Meuniere

Makes 4 servings

4 medium trout
Lemon juice
Freshly ground black pepper
2 tablespoons butter
2 tablespoons oil

¼ cup butter
¼ cup lemon juice *or* white wine
¼ cup minced fresh parsley
Sliced kiwi, avocado, mango, *or* papaya

Rub trout with lemon juice and pepper. Warm platter for fish in 200° oven. Heat butter and oil in a large frying pan over medium-high heat. Add trout and sauté until lightly browned on one side; when edges become opaque and curl slightly, 3 to 5 minutes, turn. Heat until fish flakes easily when tested with a fork in the thickest portion. Remove fish to warm platter.

Wipe out pan and melt butter. Add lemon juice and parsley all at once. Swirl and pour sauce over trout. Garnish with kiwi slices.

Variation

◆ **Trout with Lemon-Dill Sauce:** Melt ¼ cup butter; sauté 2 minced shallots or 2 tablespoons yellow onion. Add ¼ cup dry sherry, the finely grated peel of 1 lemon, and 4 minced sprigs fresh dill or fennel. Swirl and pour over trout.

Spinach Salad with Lemon-Lime Vinaigrette

Makes 4 servings

1 bunch spinach, stems removed
3 green onions, sliced
½ cup sliced radishes

1 cup bean sprouts, optional
6 to 8 cherry tomatoes, halved
Lemon-Lime Vinaigrette

Tear spinach into bite-sized pieces. Arrange other vegetables in groups on top of spinach. Serve with Lemon-Lime Vinaigrette.

Lemon-Lime Vinaigrette

Makes 1 cup

¼ cup safflower oil
2 tablespoons lemon juice

2 tablespoons lime juice
2 tablespoons minced parsley

Combine all ingredients; mix well.

Fresh Asparagus with Blender Bearnaise

Makes 4 servings

2 pounds asparagus
Boiling salted water

1 to 2 tablespoons butter
Blender Bearnaise

Wash asparagus and cut or snap off tough ends. In a wide frying pan with a little boiling water, lay spears parallel no more than three layers deep. Cook, uncovered, over high heat until stems are just tender when pierced with a fork, 6 to 8 minutes. Drain. Top with butter, and serve with Blender Bearnaise.

Note: For lighter appetites, omit Blender Bearnaise, and serve asparagus with Meuniere Sauce from Trout recipe.

Blender Bearnaise

Makes 1 cup

¼ cup wine vinegar
¼ cup vermouth *or* white wine
1 shallot *or* green onion, minced
1 teaspoon dried tarragon leaves
1 bay leaf

6 black peppercorns
6 parsley sprigs
1 cup butter
3 egg yolks

In a small saucepan, bring first 7 ingredients to a boil; reduce to 3 tablespoons. Melt butter in a separate saucepan. In blender, whirl yolks until just blended. Add reduced wine mixture and blend briefly. Add melted butter, a droplet at a time, blending continuously on high speed. As mixture thickens, increase butter to a thin stream. Keep sauce warm by placing blender container in a pan of lukewarm water, if desired.

Note: For a faster Hollandaise version, simply omit first 7 ingredients and the first step. Proceed as directed. Makes ½ cup.

Curry Bearnaise Variation

Makes 1 cup

1 tablespoon vegetable oil
½ small onion, chopped

1 tablespoon curry powder
¾ cup plain yogurt

Heat oil in skillet; sauté onion until tender. Stir in curry; cook 3 to 4 minutes, stirring constantly. Transfer to a blender or food processor. Add yogurt; blend until smooth.

Spinach Salad with Lemon-Lime Vinaigrette, Squash and Mushrooms with Herbs, page 12; Trout Meuniere, page 13; Fresh Asparagus, this page.

Confetti Scrambled Egg Pastries
Cornucopia Ham Rolls
Fruit-Filled Cantaloupe with
Lemon-Lime Cream Dressing

Frozen puff pastry shells are easy to use and their edible containers raise the humble scrambled eggs to new heights of elegance with ease. To carry on this theme of elegance, showcase summer's abundance of succulent and plump fresh fruits cascading over a cool canteloupe wedge.

Fruit-Filled Cantaloupe with Lemon-Lime Cream Dressing

Makes 4 servings

1 ripe cantaloupe, crenshaw, *or* honeydew melon

4 nectarines *or* peaches, pitted and sliced

1 tablespoon lemon juice

2 teaspoons lime juice

2 plums, pitted and sliced

½ cup blueberries

½ cup raspberries

1 kiwi fruit, peeled and sliced

Lemon-Lime Cream Dressing

Cut melon into 4 wedges; discard seeds. Coat peach slices with lemon and lime juice. Top each melon wedge with all fruits. Top with Lemon-Lime Cream Dressing.

Lemon-Lime Cream Dressing

Makes 1 cup

½ cup plain yogurt

½ cup sour cream

1 tablespoon honey

½ teaspoon dry mustard

1 teaspoon lemon juice

1 teaspoon lime juice

In a small bowl, blend all ingredients. Cover and chill until ready to use.

Confetti Scrambled Egg Pastries

Makes 4 servings

1 tablespoon vegetable oil
⅓ cup julienne cut green pepper
⅓ cup julienne cut red pepper
2 to 3 tablespoons minced onion
1 clove garlic, minced
⅓ cup salsa

¼ cup finely chopped ham
10 eggs, beaten
8 puff pastry shells, baked according to
    package directions
Salsa

In a medium skillet, heat oil and sauté green and red pepper for 1 minute. Add onion and garlic and continue sautéing until onion becomes transparent and soft. Add salsa and ham; cook 5 minutes. Stir in eggs and scramble until firm, but still moist. Serve eggs in puff pastry shells and garnish with extra salsa to taste.

Cornucopia Ham Rolls

Makes 4 servings

1 package (3 ounces) cream cheese
2 to 3 tablespoons finely chopped ginger
    preserves
½ cup finely chopped pecans

2 to 3 tablespoons milk
Freshly ground black pepper to taste
12 ham slices

Combine cheese, preserves, and pecans. Stir in milk to moisten, and season to taste. Spread over ham slices and roll up into cornucopias.

Note: Cornucopia Ham Rolls may be served on plates with Fruit-Filled Cantaloupes.

Variations

◆ **Pineapple-Yogurt Cornucopias:** Substitute ½ cup yogurt and ¼ cup chopped and drained pineapple for the cream cheese and ginger.

◆ **Curried Turkey Rolls:** Substitute turkey luncheon meat slices and 1 tablespoon curry powder for the ham and ginger.

Vegetable Fromage
Gingered Chicken with Apples
Whole Wheat Macaroni
Braised Celery Almondine
Fruited Watercress Salad

This rich chicken entrée is a healthy gourmet choice, with its unique combination of ginger and apples. A savory Cognac and cream sauce creates a velvety sensation, while the garnish of toasted almonds provides a tasty textural crunch. The Braised Celery Almondine echoes this sublimely elegant, yet nutritional, presentation.

Vegetable Fromage
Makes 4 servings

2 packages (8 ounces each) cream cheese
¼ cup plain yogurt
¼ cup shredded carrot
¼ cup finely chopped radish

¼ cup finely chopped red pepper
¼ cup finely chopped green pepper
¼ cup finely sliced green onion *or* cilantro
Whole grain breadsticks

Process all ingredients, or blend well with a wooden spoon. Use immediately or refrigerate, covered, up to 2 days. Bring to room temperature before serving with whole grain breadsticks.

Whole Wheat Macaroni
Makes 4 servings

2 quarts water
½ teaspoon salt
8 ounces elbow macaroni (whole wheat, yellow and/or green for color)

1 tablespoon oil
1 lemon stalk *or* 1 teaspoon lemon juice
Chopped fresh rosemary *or* chives

Bring water and salt to a boil. Add remaining ingredients and cook until tender but firm. Drain. Add rosemary and toss before serving.

Poached Chicken Breasts and Vermicelli in Wine, Brussels Sprouts and Creamed Carrots, page 92; Smoked Salmon a la Russe, Sherried Escarole Salad, page 90.

Gingered Chicken with Apples

Makes 4 servings

1 tablespoon safflower oil *or* vegetable oil
2½ pounds chicken, cut into pieces
¼ cup Cognac
½ cup evaporated skim milk
½ cup non-fat milk
1 tablespoon chopped gingerroot *or* ½ teaspoon ground ginger
½ teaspoon nutmeg
1½ cups thinly sliced tart apples
1 teaspoon arrowroot, optional
Toasted slivered almonds
Chopped candied ginger

Heat oil in a large skillet. Add chicken, skin side down. Brown well on all sides. Remove and set aside. Deglaze pan with Cognac. Flambé if desired. Return browned chicken to skillet. To make cream sauce, combine next 5 ingredients. Add to skillet and gently simmer, 20 to 30 minutes. Remove chicken to serving platter. Add apples to skillet. Cook until just tender, 1 to 2 minutes. Thicken with arrowroot, if desired. Serve apples and sauce over chicken. Garnish with almonds and candied ginger.

Braised Celery Almondine

Makes 4 servings

1 head celery
½ yellow onion, finely chopped
¼ cup coarsely chopped whole almonds
1 tablespoon butter
1 grated lemon peel
Minced candied ginger, optional

Separate celery into stalks and wash in boiling water. Cut diagonally into ½-inch pieces; add to boiling water (not the same used to wash the celery). Blanch 5 minutes. Drain. Meanwhile, in a large skillet, sauté onion and almonds in butter. Add lemon peel and celery. Toss to coat celery. Garnish with candied ginger.

Fruited Watercress Salad

Makes 4 servings

2 oranges, peeled and sliced
2 kiwi fruit, peeled and sliced
1 grapefruit, peeled and sliced
2 bunches watercress, tough stems removed
1 head butter lettuce, cleaned and separated into leaves
Lemon *or* lime juice
Vegetable oil

Arrange fruit on a bed of watercress and butter lettuce. Sprinkle with juice and oil to taste.

Stuffed Pea Pods
Broiled Swordfish
Lemon Dill Rice
Carrots in Lime Butter
Italian Tomato Cucumber Salad

Chevre introduces this menu; goat cheese is available domestically and from abroad. It has an earthy flavor and aroma, counterpointed by a distinctive piquant tang. It is an appropriate beginning to the Broiled Swordfish, which is characterized by its bright colors and lemony zest. The remaining recipes are designed to complement the entrée with a repeating theme of color and flavor flair.

Stuffed Pea Pods
Makes 4 servings

25 snow peas
 4 ounces mild goat cheese (Montrachet *or* Lezay)
¼ cup plain yogurt

1 teaspoon any flavored mustard
½ cup finely chopped Hot and Spicy Pecans

Cut stem ends of snow peas and pull down straight edge to remove any string. Blanch in boiling water for 30 seconds. Plunge peas into ice water. Using a sharp paring knife, slit open each pod along straight side. In bowl, combine cheese, yogurt, mustard, and ¼ cup pecans. Pipe or stuff each pea pod with goat cheese mixture. Dip stuffing side of each pod into remaining chopped nuts to garnish.

Hot and Spicy Pecans
Makes 2 cups

2 cups pecan halves
Butter, melted
Cayenne
Cumin

Paprika
Cloves
Onion salt *or* chili powder

Roast pecans in 300° oven for 20 minutes. Sprinkle with remaining ingredients to taste. Use for Stuffed Pea Pods as directed; serve balance of pecans on the side.

Lemon Dill Rice

Makes 4 servings

1 tablespoon safflower oil *or*
  vegetable oil
1 cup long-grain brown *or* white rice
1 cup finely chopped red onion
1 stalk finely chopped celery
1 large garlic clove, minced
1 can (13 ounces) low-sodium
  chicken broth

⅓ cup water
1 to 2 tablespoons lemon juice
¼ cup minced fresh dill *or*
  1 tablespoon dried dill
Freshly ground pepper
Fresh dill sprigs
Lemon slices

Heat safflower oil over medium-high heat. Add rice, onion, celery, and garlic; sauté about 5 minutes. Add broth, water, and lemon juice. Bring to a boil; reduce heat to low and simmer, covered, 20 to 30 minutes. Stir in minced dill and pepper. Remove from heat. Cover and let stand 10 minutes. Garnish with dill sprigs and lemon slices.

Carrots in Lime Butter

Makes 4 servings

1 pound carrots
4½ cups water
1 tablespoon fructose

1 to 2 tablespoons unsalted butter
2 tablespoons fresh lime juice

Cut carrots diagonally into ¼-inch thick slices. In a medium saucepan, bring carrots and 4 cups of cold water to a full boil over high heat. Boil for 3 to 5 minutes; drain. Return carrot slices to saucepan. Add ½ cup water and fructose. Bring to a boil over medium heat; cook until carrots are just tender and the liquid is reduced to 1 or 2 tablespoons, about 7 minutes. Stir in butter and lime juice.

Italian Tomato Cucumber Salad

Makes 4 servings

5 or 6 Italian-style plum tomatoes *or*
  3 large ripe tomatoes
1 stalk celery, thinly sliced
1 cucumber, sliced
3 or 4 red onions, sliced
1 clove garlic, halved

Black peppercorn
Chopped fresh oregano
Minced fresh basil
2 tablespoons olive oil *or* vegetable oil
2 tablespoons red wine vinegar

Cut tomatoes into wedges and combine with celery, cucumber, and onion. Rub a glass serving bowl with cut sides of garlic; add vegetables. Grind pepper over all and season generously with oregano and basil. Drizzle oil and vinegar evenly over salad; toss gently. Serve at room temperature.

Broiled Swordfish, page 24; Lemon Dill Rice, Carrots in Lime Butter, Italian Tomato Cucumber Salad, this page.

Broiled Swordfish

Makes 4 servings

Freshly ground pepper
4 1¾-pound swordfish *or* halibut steaks,
  cut 1 inch thick
1 tablespoon butter
1 large red pepper, cut into
  julienne strips
1 large green pepper, cut into
  julienne strips

4 tablespoons lemon juice
¼ cup grated Parmesan cheese
2 tablespoons chopped fresh basil,
  optional
Lemon wedges

Preheat broiler to high. Grind pepper generously over swordfish. Heat butter over medium-high heat; add peppers and sauté until tender and well-browned, about 10 minutes. Set aside. Broil swordfish 4 to 5 inches from heat source for about 3 minutes. Sprinkle 2 tablespoons of lemon juice evenly over steaks. Turn fish, sprinkle remaining juice, and broil for 5 minutes more, or until fish flakes easily when tested with a fork. Spread peppers evenly over swordfish; sprinkle with Parmesan cheese and basil. Garnish with lemon wedges.

Dill-Cucumber Variation

½ cucumber, diced
½ small red onion, diced
1 tablespoon Dijon-style mustard

½ cup plain yogurt
½ cup cream cheese
2 tablespoons minced fresh dillweed

Omit butter, peppers, Parmesan cheese, and basil. Broil Swordfish as directed. In a small bowl, combine variation ingredients; blend well. Serve with Broiled Swordfish. *Note:* Dill-Cucumber Sauce can be prepared 1 to 2 days in advance. Combine all ingredients, except onion and cucumber. Refrigerate. Stir in cucumber and onion just before serving.

Fruit with Honey Dip
Chicken Jambalaya Stir-Fry
Broiled Sourdough Slices
Tomato, Carrot, and Orange Salad

*This Creole-style paella is easiest to make, and serve, from
your wok. The exciting ethnic flavors in this entrée
are elevated when accompanied by sourdough and a salad
with a citrus zest.*

Fruit with Honey Dip
Makes 1 cup

1 tablespoon honey
½ cup Neufchatel cheese *or* ricotta
   cheese
½ cup plain yogurt

Grated peel of ½ lime *or* ½ lemon
Grated peel of ½ orange
1 tablespoon jam *or* preserves
Choice of fruits

Combine all ingredients; mix well. Serve as a dip with your favorite fruits, prepared
in bite-sized pieces.

Tomato, Carrot, and Orange Salad
Makes 4 servings

4 lettuce leaves
4 large tomatoes, cut into wedges
2 large carrots, grated
⅔ cup peanut oil
   Juice and grated rind of one orange

1 tablespoon red wine vinegar
1 teaspoon Dijon-style mustard
1 teaspoon sugar
   Salt and freshly ground black pepper
   Orange wedges

Line 4 bowls with lettuce leaves, and top with tomatoes and carrots. Combine remaining ingredients. Pour dressing over each salad just before serving, and serve the
balance on the side. Garnish with orange wedges.

Chicken Jambalaya Stir-Fry

Makes 4 servings

2 to 3 cloves garlic, minced
½ cup chopped red onion
1 stalk celery, sliced
2 hot chorizos, casings removed and
  broken up
2 tablespoons olive oil *or* vegetable oil
1 cup chicken broth
1 cup white wine
1 cup long-grain white rice

1 can (16 ounces) stewed tomatoes,
  chopped
1 teaspoon thyme *or* oregano leaves
½ teaspoon turmeric
¼ teaspoon red pepper
½ package (20 ounces) frozen peas
1 pound medium-sized raw shrimp,
  in shells *or* frozen shrimp

Sauté first 4 ingredients, 3 to 5 minutes in hot oil. Add next 7 ingredients. Bring to a boil. Reduce heat; cover and simmer 15 minutes. Add peas and shrimp. Cover and cook 5 minutes. Toss with a fork to fluff rice and distribute shrimp.
Note: 8 fresh mussels or clams may be substituted for ½ pound of shrimp.

Broiled Sourdough Slices

Makes 4 servings

½ loaf sourdough French bread
½ cup butter, softened
2 to 3 cloves garlic, minced

¼ cup minced fresh parsley
¼ cup freshly grated Romano *or*
  Parmesan cheese

Preheat broiler. Slice French bread. Blend remaining ingredients and spread evenly over bread slices. Broil until golden and bubbly.

Chicken Sourdough Variation

½ cup green pepper strips
1 tablespoon butter
1½ to 2 cups cooked chicken
¼ cup sliced olives

2 to 3 tablespoons tomato paste
½ teaspoon chopped fresh basil
½ teaspoon chopped fresh thyme

Sauté peppers in butter; remove from heat. Stir in remaining ingredients. Spread over sourdough slices. Sprinkle with cheese and broil as directed.

Tomato, Carrot, and Orange Salad, Fruit with Honey Dip, page 25; Broiled Sourdough Slices, Chicken Jambalaya Stir-Fry, this page.
***Overleaf:** Dilled Shrimp on Avocados, page 30; Individual Beef Wellingtons, Potato Bake Chantilly, page 31; Butter-Steamed Spinach with Lemon-Lime Mayonnaise, Spicy Tomato Soup, page 32.*

Dilled Shrimp on Avocados
Individual Beef Wellingtons
Potato Bake Chantilly
Butter-Steamed Spinach
with Lemon-Lime Mayonnaise
Spicy Tomato Soup

This shrimp appetizer is marvelous on toast rounds or in pita bread pockets, as well as in an avocado. In this menu, however, the avocado provides a cool and colorful contrast to the hearty meat and potatoes theme and accents the Spicy Tomato Soup.

Dilled Shrimp on Avocados

Makes 4 servings

3 tablespoons cream cheese, softened
3 tablespoons mayonnaise
1 teaspoon lemon juice
⅛ to ¼ teaspoon dried dillweed
1 tablespoon minced parsley
2 tablespoons minced green onion

1 pound small bay shrimp, cooked
2 avocados, halved
4 butter lettuce leaves
4 sprigs green onion
4 cherry tomatoes

Cream first 4 ingredients. Fold in parsley, onion, and shrimp. Cover and refrigerate at least 30 minutes. Top each avocado half with an equal portion of shrimp mixture. Serve on lettuce leaf. Garnish with green onion and tomato.

Variation

◆ **Low-Cal:** Omit cream cheese and mayonnaise. Add ½ cup plain yogurt *or* ½ cup creamed cottage cheese.

Individual Beef Wellingtons

Makes 4 servings

4 filet mignons, 1½ inches thick
1 box (10 ounces) frozen puff pastry sheets, thawed
1 egg yolk, slightly beaten
1 tablespoon water
1 tablespoon butter

¾ pound mushrooms, diced
⅓ cup minced green onion *or* shallots
⅓ cup parsley
¼ cup port *or* Madeira
¼ cup Dijon-style mustard

Pan-fry or broil meat 1½ minutes per side; set aside. Reserve ¼ of a puff pastry sheet; roll out remaining pastry into four rounds. Mix egg and water; set aside. Melt butter in a heavy skillet; sauté mushrooms, onions, and parsley until just tender, and flambé with port. Place one pastry round on lightly floured surface. Spread with 1 tablespoon mustard and ¼ of mushroom mixture. Place filet on top and wrap tightly like a Christmas package; flip over. Cut leaves and flowers out of reserved pastry sheet, and decorate top of Wellington. Brush with egg mixture. Repeat with remaining filets. Bake in 450° oven until pastry is golden, 10 to 15 minutes.

Potato Bake Chantilly

Makes 4 servings

2 large potatoes, coarsely diced
1 small onion, quartered
1 bay leaf
1 stalk celery, sliced
3½ cups water
2 eggs, separated

Salt and pepper to taste
1 to 2 tablespoons minced chives *or* parsley
½ cup whipping cream, whipped
¼ cup grated low-fat Farmers cheese *or* Parmesan cheese

Combine potatoes, onion, bay leaf, celery, and water in a large saucepan; cook until tender, about 20 minutes. Drain; reserve 1 cup of cooking liquid. Discard bay leaf and mash cooked vegetables with 1 cup of reserved liquid until creamy. Add egg yolks. Season to taste with salt and pepper; pour into a lightly oiled baking dish. Beat egg whites until they hold stiff peaks. Fold in whipped cream and spread over the potato mixture. Sprinkle with grated cheese and place in preheated 500° oven. Turn heat down to 325° immediately; bake until heated through and lightly browned.

Variation

◆ **Buttery Chantilly:** Omit cheese. Dot with ¼ cup unsalted butter. Bake as directed.

Butter-Steamed Spinach with Lemon-Lime Mayonnaise

Makes 4 servings

1¼ to 1½ pounds spinach
1 tablespoon butter

2 tablespoons water
Lemon-Lime Mayonnaise

Slice spinach stems diagonally and chop leaves roughly. Melt butter in a large heavy skillet. Add stems; cover and cook 3 to 4 minutes. Add leaves and sprinkle with water. Cover and cook 3 to 4 minutes longer. Serve with Lemon-Lime Mayonnaise.

Lemon-Lime Mayonnaise

Makes 1 cup

⅔ cup mayonnaise, at room temperature
Juice of ½ lemon
Juice of ½ lime

1 teaspoon Worcestershire sauce
Salt and freshly ground pepper

Combine all ingredients; blend well and adjust seasonings to taste.

Spicy Tomato Soup

Makes 4 generous servings

1 tablespoon butter
1 red onion, minced
1 can (16 ounces) tomatoes,
coarsely crushed
2 cups chicken broth
1 teaspoon paprika
½ teaspoon sugar
½ teaspoon basil
½ bay leaf

¼ teaspoon chili powder
Dash cloves
⅛ teaspoon nutmeg
¼ cup minced parsley
3 avocados, diced, reserve 4 heaping
tablespoons
Lemon slices
Sour cream

Melt butter in a large pot. Add onion; cover and cook until transparent, about 5 minutes. Add tomatoes, broth, paprika, sugar, basil, bay leaf, chili powder, cloves, and nutmeg. Cover and simmer for 15 minutes. Remove from heat and discard bay leaf. Just before serving, stir in parsley and avocado. Garnish each serving with a lemon slice, sour cream, and a heaping tablespoon of diced avocado.

Variation

◆ **Parmesan Tomato Soup**: Omit basil, bay leaf, and nutmeg. Just before serving, stir in ¼ to ½ cup Parmesan cheese.

> **Bright Borscht**
> **Breakfast Croissant Sandwiches**
> **Fruited Bibb Salad with**
> **Yogurt Dressing**

*These croissants are definitely a staircase above anything
served in fast-food drive-through restaurants. Prepare
ingredients in advance, and allow guests to
create their own croissants.*

Fruited Bibb Salad
Makes 4 servings

2 small heads Bibb *or* butterhead lettuce Yogurt Dressing
½ avocado, sliced
2 oranges, peeled, seeded, and sliced
   into rounds

Separate lettuce into leaves. Arrange avocado and orange slices attractively over lettuce. Top with Yogurt Dressing.

Note: Slices of peaches, papaya, nectarines, or grapefruit may be substituted for oranges.

Yogurt Dressing
Makes 1 cup

1 cup plain yogurt   Fructose to taste
¼ cup orange juice   Dash ground cloves
2 teaspoons grated orange peel

Stir all ingredients together. Let dressing stand at least 15 minutes to blend flavors.

Variation

◆ **Ginger Yogurt:** Omit orange peel and cloves. Add ½ teaspoon minced fresh ginger.

Bright Borscht

Makes 4 servings

1 pound cooked beets, sliced, fresh *or* canned
1 can (14½ ounces) low-sodium chicken broth
¼ cup coarsely chopped red onion
1 clove garlic

3 to 4 tablespoons orange juice
½ cup plain yogurt *or* Neufchatel cheese, softened
1 cucumber, diced
Orange slices

Process or blend first 5 ingredients until smooth. Stir in yogurt and cucumber. Chill and garnish with orange slices before serving.

Breakfast Croissant Sandwiches

Makes 4 servings

4 croissants, warmed and split in half
4 omelets (page 49)

4 large mushrooms, thinly sliced
12 avocado slices

Layer all ingredients into croissants.

Variations

◆ **Ham and cheese:** Substitute omelets and mushrooms with 8 ounces sliced ham, 4 slices Swiss cheese, and 8 ounces sliced pineapple.

◆ **BLT:** Substitute omelets and mushrooms with 8 cooked bacon strips, 4 lettuce leaves, and 4 tomato slices.

English Muffin Variation

4 English muffins, split
¼ cup butter
4 omelets (page 49)

4 large mushrooms, thinly sliced
12 avocado slices

Toast muffins; spread with butter. Top with remaining ingredients. Serve open-faced.

Fruited Bibb Salad with Yogurt Dressing, page 33;
Breakfast Croissant Sandwiches, Bright Borscht, this page.

Crab-Stuffed Mushrooms
Mustard-Broiled Pork Chops
Pasta and Garlic
Carrots Purée in Zucchini Shells
Grilled Goat Cheese and Walnut Salad
with Mango Dressing

*Do you know anyone who doesn't like crab, cheese, and
mushrooms? Watch these appetizers disappear at your
next party. They'll be followed quickly by
these other Fast and Fresh recipes.*

Crab-Stuffed Mushrooms

Makes 4 servings

3 tablespoons butter
12 large mushroom caps
2 cloves garlic, minced
½ cup Monterey Jack *or* mozzarella
   cheese, shredded
1 can (6 ounces) flaked crab

2 tablespoons red *or* white wine
1 to 2 teaspoons Worcestershire sauce
2 tablespoons fine dry bread crumbs
   Freshly ground pepper
   Shredded Monterey Jack cheese

Melt 1 tablespoon butter in sauté pan. Sauté mushroom caps, coating well with butter.
Combine remaining butter and next 6 ingredients until blended. Place mushrooms
on rimmed baking sheet. Evenly mound filling into each mushroom cavity, pressing
lightly. Sprinkle with pepper and cheese. Broil about 6 inches from heat source, 5 to 8
minutes. Serve immediately.

Mustard-Broiled Pork Chops

Makes 4 servings

¼ cup Dijon-style *or* imported mustard
4 pork loin chops, ¾ inch thick, trimmed

Freshly ground pepper to taste

Preheat broiler. Spread half of the mustard evenly over chops. Broil 6 inches away
from heat source for 8 to 10 minutes. Turn chops; spread with remaining mustard.
Grind pepper over chops. Broil another 10 minutes.

Pasta and Garlic

Makes 4 servings

2 cups chicken broth
2 cups water
½ pound fresh pasta
1 tablespoon butter
2 cloves garlic, minced

¼ cup minced fresh parsley
1 teaspoon basil, marjoram, oregano, *or* thyme
Freshly grated Parmesan, Romano, *or* Sapsago cheese

Bring broth and water to a boil in a large pot. Add pasta and cook until tender but still firm, 4 to 6 minutes. Drain and transfer to a heated platter. Melt butter in a small saucepan and stir in garlic, parsley, and herbs. Heat gently. Pour parsley mixture over noodles and toss to coat well. Garnish with grated cheese.

Carrots Purée in Zucchini Shells

Makes 4 servings

1 tablespoon butter
1 pound carrots, thinly sliced
3 tablespoons water
½ cup evaporated skim milk

1 to 2 tablespoons dry sherry
¼ teaspoon nutmeg
¼ teaspoon cinnamon
4 medium zucchini, baked until soft

Melt butter in large skillet; add carrots and water. Steam, covered, until tender, 5 to 8 minutes. In a blender, combine carrots with next 5 ingredients; blend until smooth. Split zucchini lengthwise and scoop out seeds. Spoon carrot purée into each zucchini shell, or pipe, using a pastry bag fitted with a rosette tip.

Grilled Goat Cheese and Walnut Salad with Mango Dressing

Makes 4 servings

1 head radicchio
1 head butter lettuce
1 head Arugula
4 to 6 ounces mild herbed goat cheese
½ cup walnut *or* hazelnut oil *or* vegetable oil

1 tablespoon mango chutney
1 tablespoon plain yogurt
2 teaspoons red wine vinegar
1 cup coarsely chopped walnuts

Discard any outer leaves, then wash and pat dry all greens. Refrigerate. Slice cheese into four chunks. Grill or broil briefly and set aside. Process or blend next 4 ingredients for dressing. To compose salad, arrange lettuce leaves on a platter. Form a ring of Arugula over lettuce. Place cheese, pinwheel fashion, in center. Sprinkle with walnuts and drizzle on dressing.

> Herring Canapés
> Beef Filet with Mushroom Bordelaise and Tomato
> Creamy Linguine
> Sautéed Cabbage and Peas
> Glazed Parsnips
> Endive and Asparagus Salad
> with Sherried Mustard Dressing

Filet mignon is the cut traditionally used in this menu, but less expensive cuts, such as flank, top round, and chuck can be substituted. Reduce cooking time on these cuts by 4 to 6 minutes on each side for rare meat. The firmer the steak, the more well-done it is. If you choose to grill the steaks outdoors over coals, allow extra time to prepare coals for cooking.

Sautéed Cabbage and Peas
Makes 4 servings

1 teaspoon butter
2½ cups raw cabbage, shredded
10 ounces frozen petite peas

Nutmeg to taste
White pepper to taste

Melt butter in a large skillet and sauté cabbage until slightly wilted, about 3 minutes. Add peas and seasonings; cook, stirring, until heated through, 3 to 5 minutes.

Endive and Asparagus Salad
with Sherried Mustard Dressing
Makes 4 servings

10 asparagus spears, steamed
2 heads endive, torn *or* 1 head
escarole, torn
2 green onions, chopped

½ cup plain yogurt
1½ teaspoons Dijon-style mustard
1 to 2 tablespoons dry sherry

Arrange asparagus spears over endive. Mix together onion, yogurt, mustard, and sherry. Spoon over salad.

Mustard-Broiled Pork Chops, page 36; Pasta and Garlic,
Carrots Purée in Zucchini Shells, Grilled Goat Cheese
and Walnut Salad with Mango Dressing, page 37.

Herring Canapés

Makes 4 servings

1 large cucumber
1 loaf (8 ounces) party rye bread, sliced
2 teaspoons butter, softened

1 jar (12 ounces) herring in sour cream
Paprika
Dillweed sprigs

Score cucumber by running a fork down the length of the cucumber from end to end. Cut crosswise into very thin slices. Place in a bowl of salted ice water and let stand in freezer 10 minutes. Drain on paper towel. Spread bread slices with butter. Overlap 2 cucumber slices on each slice of bread. Top with 1 large or 2 small pieces of herring. Sprinkle with paprika and garnish with a sprig of dillweed.

Beef Filet with Mushroom Bordelaise and Tomato

Makes 4 servings

4 filet mignon steaks, 1½ to 2 inches thick

2 large tomatoes, sliced
Mushroom Bordelaise

Preheat broiler. About 20 minutes before serving, place steaks on broiler 4 inches away from heat source. Broil 7 to 8 minutes per side for rare meat. To serve, place each steak on top of 1 or 2 slices of tomato. Top with Mushroom Bordelaise.

Mushroom Bordelaise

Makes 4 servings

½ pound mushrooms, sliced
¼ cup shallots, chopped
1 teaspoon safflower oil *or* vegetable oil
1 teaspoon butter

Juice from ½ lemon
¼ cup parsley, minced
¼ cup Madeira *or* port

Sauté mushrooms and shallots in oil and butter, 2 to 3 minutes. Quickly stir in lemon juice and parsley. Flambé with Madeira or port.

Tofu Bearnaise Variation

7 ounces tofu, softened
2 tablespoons apple cider vinegar
2 tablespoons safflower oil *or* vegetable oil

Dash pepper
3 tablespoons Dijon-style mustard
2 teaspoons fresh lemon juice

Combine all ingredients in a food processor or blender. Blend at high speed until smooth.

Creamy Linguine

Makes 4 servings

2 quarts water
1 teaspoon salt, optional
8 ounces linguine *or* egg noodles, thin or medium

2 tablespoons Neufchatel cheese
1 tablespoon plain yogurt
2 tablespoons poppy seeds, optional

Bring water and salt to a boil. Add noodles and cook, uncovered, until tender but firm, 4 to 8 minutes. Drain. Warm Neufchatel and yogurt in the same pan. Add noodles and poppy seeds, if desired, and toss gently to mix.

Variations

◆ **Extra Cheese:** Sprinkle with ¼ to ½ cup freshly grated Parmesan cheese. Toss to coat.

◆ **Alfredo:** Sauté 2 to 3 cloves minced garlic in 1 tablespoon butter. Add to prepared linguine. Omit poppy seeds. Sprinkle with ¼ to ½ cup minced parsley, ¼ cup grated Parmesan cheese, and a dash of ground nutmeg; toss.

◆ **Mushroom:** Sauté ¼ pound sliced fresh mushrooms in 1 to 2 tablespoons butter. Add to prepared linguine and toss.

Glazed Parsnips

Makes 4 servings

1 pound (6 to 8) medium parsnips
2 tablespoons butter

2 tablespoons brandy
1 tablespoon brown sugar *or* honey

Cover parsnips with water in a large skillet; boil until just tender, 10 to 15 minutes. Drain and add remaining ingredients. Sauté over medium-high heat 5 minutes, shaking pan occasionally to glaze parsnips on all sides.

> Crabmeat Canapés
> Veal and Artichoke Sauté
> Fresh Herb Pasta
> Sautéed Vegetable Medley
> Chilled Cream of Watercress Soup

*Zippy Crabmeat Canapés are easy to prepare and easy to eat.
The light hors d'oeuvre is a dramatic contrast to the
Veal and Artichoke Sauté, which is prepared in the classic
Cordon Bleu style, with butter, wine, and cream. The
Watercress Soup is a very well-received recipe that serves to
compromise the light and heavy spectrum of this menu.*

Crabmeat Canapés

Makes 4 servings

1 can (4 ounces) crabmeat, well drained
2 tablespoons mayonnaise
2 tablespoons plain yogurt
1 tablespoon minced chives
1 tablespoon parsley
1 teaspoon lime juice
1 teaspoon Worcestershire sauce
Freshly ground black pepper to taste
Melba toast rounds

Combine all ingredients, except toast rounds; blend well. Spread on toast rounds and serve immediately.

Veal and Artichoke Sauté

Makes 4 servings

1 pound veal, chicken breasts, *or* turkey cutlets, cut to finger lengths
Flour
Salt and pepper
½ teaspoon sage
2 tablespoons butter
1 package (9 ounces) frozen artichoke hearts, thawed
½ cup dry white wine *or* vermouth
½ cup chicken broth
¼ cup half-and-half *or* whipping cream
Grated Parmesan cheese

Dust veal lightly with flour and seasonings. Sauté in butter over medium-high heat 4 to 6 minutes. Transfer to serving platter and keep warm. Add artichokes, wine, broth, and half-and-half to skillet. Cover and simmer until artichokes are tender. Pour over veal and dust with cheese.

Fresh Herb Pasta
Makes 4 servings

2 quarts water
1 teaspoon salt
8 ounces wide *or* medium fresh noodles
1 tablespoon oil

Freshly ground black pepper
2 tablespoons chopped fresh rosemary,
thyme, *or* chives

Bring water and salt to a boil. Add noodles and oil; cook until tender but firm, 5 to 8 minutes. Drain. Toss with pepper and rosemary before serving.

Sautéed Vegetable Medley
Makes 4 servings

¾ pound small new potatoes, quartered
Water
1 teaspoon salt
1 large carrot, cut in sticks
4 small white onions, halved
2 tablespoons butter

½ pound mushrooms, halved
1 teaspoon lemon juice
1 teaspoon dried basil
Grated Parmesan, Romano, *or* Sapsago
cheese, optional

In a large kettle, cover potatoes with water; add salt and boil until tender, about 10 minutes. After 5 minutes, add carrots and onions. Melt butter in a large skillet; sauté mushrooms. Drain boiled vegetables and sauté briefly with mushrooms. Add lemon juice and basil; toss to mix. Garnish with cheese, if desired.

Chilled Cream of Watercress Soup
Makes 4 servings

2 tablespoons butter
1 bunch green onions, chopped
2 tablespoons flour
2 tablespoons nonfat dry milk
1 quart half-and-half, at room
temperature
2 bunches watercress, roughly chopped
(reserve 4 sprigs for garnish)

¼ teaspoon nutmeg
2 teaspoons lemon juice
Salt and freshly ground pepper
Yogurt
Lemon wheels

Melt butter in saucepan; sauté onion briefly. Stir in flour and dry milk; blend and cook until bubbly. Gradually add half-and-half. Cook, stirring continuously, until soup comes to a boil and thickens. Reduce heat; simmer. Add watercress, nutmeg, and lemon juice. Cover and simmer 3 minutes. Remove soup from heat and whirl in blender until smooth. Season to taste and chill. Garnish each serving with yogurt, a watercress sprig, and lemon wheels.

Overleaf: Veal and Artichoke Sauté, page 42; Fresh Herb Pasta, Sautéed Vegetable Medley, Chilled Cream of Watercress Soup, this page.

Figs and Fruit with Parma Ham
Fillets of Fish in Papaya Beurre Blanc
Almond Rice
Fresh Vegetable Salad with
Yogurt Chive Dressing

Almond Rice is delectable when served with this piquant papaya sauce. Sweet parsnips and a Yogurt Chive Dressing heighten the intensity of flavors and colors throughout this array of recipes.

Figs and Fruit with Parma Ham
Makes 4 servings

 4 slices honeydew melon
 4 slices cantaloupe *or* Cassaba melon
 4 fresh figs, washed and trimmed
12 thin slices Parma ham *or* Westphalian
     or prosciutto

Ground *or* minced candied ginger, optional

Fill four shallow soup bowls with crushed ice. Wrap each melon slice with a slice of ham; distribute among bowls. Wrap each fig with a slice of ham; center on melon slices. Serve with a dish of ginger, if desired.

Almond Rice
Makes 4 servings

 2 cups water
¼ teaspoon salt
 1 cup white rice

 1 tablespoon butter
 1 bag (2½ ounces) sliced almonds

Bring water, salt, and rice to a boil. Cover, reduce heat, and simmer until water is absorbed, about 20 minutes. Melt butter in a small skillet; when frothy, add almonds and sauté until lightly browned. Stir almonds into rice before serving.

Fillets of Fish in Papaya Beurre Blanc, Fresh Vegetable Salad with Yogurt Chive Dressing, page 48; Almond Rice, Fruit with Parma Ham, this page.

Fillets of Fish in Papaya Beurre Blanc

Makes 4 servings

1 teaspoon butter
1 teaspoon oil
1¼ pounds fish fillets (sea bass, snapper, cod, *or* flounder)
1 large papaya *or* mango, diced
¼ cup dry white wine

2 to 3 tablespoons white wine vinegar
½ teaspoon thyme leaves *or* basil
3 tablespoons lemon juice
½ pound unsalted butter, melted
Salt and freshly ground pepper to taste

Heat butter and oil in saucepan over medium-high heat. Sauté fillets, rounded side first, until deep golden brown, 2 to 3 minutes per side. Transfer to serving platter and keep warm.

To prepare Papaya Beurre Blanc, place papaya, wine, vinegar, thyme, and lemon juice in a medium saucepan; bring to a boil. Lower heat and simmer slowly until mixture is reduced by half. Blend or process papaya mixture 1½ minutes. With machine running, add melted butter in a thin stream. Season to taste with salt and pepper; strain. Serve over warm fish fillets.

Fresh Vegetable Salad with Yogurt Chive Dressing

Makes 4 servings

1 bunch watercress
1 carrot
1 crookneck squash

1 cucumber, thinly sliced
¼ cup sliced ripe olives
Yogurt Chive Dressing

Remove tough stems from watercress and arrange on plate. Cut carrot and squash into long, thin strips using a vegetable peeler; gently mix with cucumber and olives. Mound on watercress and top with Yogurt Chive Dressing.

Yogurt Chive Dressing

Makes ¾ cup

½ cup plain yogurt
1 green onion, finely chopped
2 teaspoons chopped fresh chives *or*
  ½ teaspoon dried chives

1 teaspoon lemon juice

Combine all ingredients; mix well and chill to blend flavors.

> **Fig Tulips with Ricotta Cream**
> **Open Omelet Variations**
> **Fresh Herb Scones**
> **Apple Slaw**

This menu is an inspiration in cooking. The fancy Fig Tulips can be prepared in advance. A bouquet of topping variations turns everyday omelets into stunning entreés. Fresh Scones are simple and savory. And finally, the Apple Slaw is an exceptional blend of flavors and nutritional low calories.

Open Omelet Variations

Makes 4 servings

4 eggs, separated
¼ teaspoon salt
¼ teaspoon cream of tartar

2 tablespoons water
1 to 2 teaspoons butter
½ to 1 cup topping of your choice

Preheat oven to 350°. Beat egg whites with salt and cream of tartar at high speed until stiff, but not dry. Beat yolks with water at high speed until thick and lemon-colored, about 5 minutes. Fold yolks into whites. Heat butter in 10-inch omelet pan over medium heat until just hot enough to sizzle a drop of water. Pour in omelet mixture and carefully smooth the surface. Cook until puffy and lightly browned on the bottom, about 5 minutes. Bake in oven for about 10 minutes, or until a knife inserted in the center comes out clean. Cover surface with chosen topping. Cut in half or in wedges to serve. Garnish as desired.

Topping Variations

◆ **Italian Sausage**: Cook, drain, and crumble 2 Italian sausages. Combine with 1 large tomato, diced, and 2 tablespoons chopped fresh basil *or* 1 tablespoon dried basil. Ladle over omelet; sprinkle with grated Romano.

◆ **Light Lox**: Drain and chop 2 slices smoked salmon (lox). Combine with 4 ounces Neufchatel cheese until mixed. Spread on omelet. Sprinkle omelet with lemon juice and chopped chives.

◆ **Healthy Melissa Crisp Vegetable-Garden Patch**: Sauté or steam 1 cup sliced fresh vegetables of your choice. Garnish with lemon wedges.

Fig Tulips with Ricotta Cream

Makes 4 servings

12 medium-large ripe fresh figs
½ cup ricotta cheese
½ cup cream cheese
½ teaspoon lemon rind

½ teaspoon orange rind
½ teaspoon vanilla
3 to 4 tablespoons powdered sugar
12 unblanched whole almonds

Rinse figs and pat dry. Trim off stems. Cut each fig into 4 petals by cutting through fig from stem end to within ½ inch of other end. (Cover and chill if made ahead.) Process or blend remaining ingredients, except almonds. Stand 2 to 3 figs upright on each plate. Gently open each fig and spoon in about 2 tablespoons of cheese mixture. Top each with an almond.

Fresh Herb Scones

Makes 4 servings

2 cups all-purpose unbleached flour
½ cup whole wheat flour
1 to 2 teaspoons fructose
2 teaspoons baking powder
1 teaspoon crushed rosemary
1 teaspoon baking soda

1 teaspoon salt
1 teaspoon thyme
1 teaspoon oregano
¼ cup butter
1 egg (reserve 1 tablespoon white)
½ cup plus 2 tablespoons buttermilk

Preheat oven to 400°. Combine or blend first 9 ingredients in bowl or food processor. Cut butter into small pieces and work into flour mixture with food processor or pastry blender, until blended. In a separate bowl, beat egg with buttermilk and stir into mixture. Turn dough out on a floured board and knead for 2 minutes. Shape into 2 thick circles, 5 inches in diameter. Cut each into quarters and place on lightly greased baking sheet with wedges about ½ inch apart. Brush with reserved egg white. Bake for 15 to 20 minutes or until nicely browned. Serve warm.

Apple Slaw

Makes 4 servings

⅓ cup plain yogurt
¼ cup sour half-and-half or sour cream
2 to 3 tablespoons minced chives
1 tablespoon lemon juice
1 teaspoon lime juice
1 tablespoon minced cilantro or parsley

1 teaspoon grated lemon rind
Salt to taste
Freshly ground pepper to taste
1 large red apple
1 cup grated, peeled celery root
1 cup grated, peeled jicama or turnip

In a large bowl, mix first 7 ingredients. Season to taste with salt and freshly ground pepper. Core apple but do not peel. Grate apple and add to yogurt mixture at once to keep apples from browning. Apple peel that does not pass through grater can be finely chopped. Blend in celery root and jicama. Let stand at room temperature for 30 minutes to blend.

*Open Omelet with Italian Sausage Topping Variation,
page 49; Fresh Herb Scones, Apple Slaw, this page.*

Huevos with Salsa Verde
(Eggs with Watercress Mayonnaise)
Foiled Fish with Salsa
Fiesta Rice
Lemon Chayote Sauté
Cabbage Succotash

This foiled fish dish is an adaption of a dramatic entrée discovered in Ixtapa, Mexico — the fish actually poaches in its own juices. Lemon Chayote Sauté is a delicious complement — this vegetable pear has a nutty, pear-apple flavor, which also works well as a contrast to the spicy Cabbage Succotash.

Foiled Fish with Salsa
Makes 4 servings

4 1 to 1½-pound fish fillets (snapper,
  cod, sea bass, *or* orange roughy fillets)
½ cup thick salsa

8 large shrimp
Cilantro sprigs *or* parsley
1 lime, cut into wedges

Cut foil or parchment paper into 8 heart-shaped pieces 1 inch longer than fillets. Place a fillet on each heart; top with 2 tablespoons salsa, 2 shrimp, and 1 or 2 cilantro sprigs. Cover with another foil heart; seal edges. Bake at 400° for 10 to 12 minutes. Transfer to dinner plates. Cut a large "X" in each foil packet; turn back foil to expose fish. Garnish with lime wedges and serve steaming hot.

Cabbage Succotash
Makes 4 servings

1 tablespoon lard *or* safflower oil *or*
  vegetable oil
4 cups sliced green *or* Napa cabbage
1 can (4 ounces) diced green chilies
1 package (10 ounces) frozen corn,
  thawed

1 large tomato, chopped *or* 1 jar
  (2 ounces) diced pimientos
Salt and freshly ground pepper to taste

Melt lard in a large skillet. Sauté cabbage over medium-high heat for 3 minutes, or until slightly wilted. Add remaining ingredients and cook, stirring continuously, until heated through, 3 to 5 minutes.

Huevos with Salsa Verde
(Eggs with Watercress Mayonnaise)
Makes 4 servings

8 hard-boiled eggs, halved
½ pound cooked baby shrimp *or* prawns
Cucumber slices

Watercress Mayonnaise
Watercress sprigs
Lemon wedges

Divide egg halves, shrimp, and cucumber slices evenly among 4 serving dishes. Pour mayonnaise evenly over eggs and garnish with watercress and lemon wedges.

Watercress Mayonnaise
Makes 1⅓ cups

1 egg
2 tablespoons white wine vinegar *or* lemon juice
½ cup watercress sprigs
½ cup parsley sprigs
1 green onion, sliced

2 teaspoons Dijon-style mustard
½ teaspoon tarragon leaves
½ cup safflower oil *or* vegetable oil
½ cup Neufchatel cheese *or* kefir
Salt and freshly ground pepper to taste

Combine first 7 ingredients in a blender or food processor; blend until smooth. With machine running, add oil, a few drops at a time, increasing flow to a slow, steady stream. Blend in cheese and season with salt and pepper.

Fiesta Rice
Makes 4 servings

1 tablespoon butter
½ cup finely chopped onion
1 to 2 cloves garlic, minced
¼ cup diced green chilies
1 16-ounce can stewed tomatoes

Salt and pepper to taste
3 cups cooked rice
Sour half-and-half, optional
Jalapeno chilies, optional

Melt butter in skillet over medium-high heat and cook onion until soft. Add next 6 ingredients and simmer, about 15 minutes. Garnish with sour half-and-half and sliced jalapeno chilies, if desired.

Lemon Chayote Sauté
Makes 4 servings

2 to 3 chayotes, peeled, halved, and thinly sliced
1 teaspoon butter

1 teaspoon safflower oil *or* vegetable oil
¼ cup grated Parmesan cheese
¼ cup minced fresh parsley

Sauté chayotes in butter and oil over medium heat until tender-crisp, about 5 minutes. Stir in Parmesan cheese and parsley; sauté on high heat until Parmesan just begins to turn golden.

Pecan-Gilded Camembert
Lemon-Stuffed Veal
Spiced Mushroom Pilaf
Green Beans Provencal
Cream of Zucchini Soup with Crabmeat
Braised Celery and Red Peppers

*Pecan-Gilded Camembert is an elegant, classic appetizer,
and a year-round favorite; however, holiday colors do prevail
when red and green apples are used. It also enhances
these traditional variations on stuffed veal,
mushroom pilaf, and Green Beans Provencal.*

Pecan-Gilded Camembert

Makes 4 servings

1 whole (7 to 8 ounces) firm Camembert
   or Brie cheese
2 tablespoons butter, melted
2 tablespoons brown sugar

1 cup pecan *or* walnut halves
Red and green apple wedges
Pears *or* bread sticks

Preheat oven to 350°. Place cheese in a 10-inch or 11-inch round baking dish. Brush cheese with butter and sprinkle with sugar. Arrange nuts on top. Bake 10 to 12 minutes. Serve on a warming tray with apples, pears, or bread sticks.

Spiced Mushroom Pilaf

Makes 4 servings

½ tablespoon butter
¼ cup minced red onion
1 cup sliced mushrooms
1 clove garlic, minced
1 cup white rice
1 tablespoon minced fresh ginger *or*
   ½ teaspoon ground ginger

½ teaspoon paprika
⅛ teaspoon turmeric
2 cups water
Freshly ground pepper

Melt butter in a large saucepan. Sauté onions, mushrooms, and garlic until softened, 3 to 5 minutes. Add remaining ingredients. Bring to a boil. Reduce heat; cover and simmer until all water is absorbed, about 20 minutes.

*Lemon-Stuffed Veal, Cream of Zucchini Soup with
Crabmeat, page 56; Green Beans Provencal, page 57;
Pecan-Gilded Camembert, Spiced Mushroom Pilaf, this page.*

Lemon-Stuffed Veal

Makes 4 servings

1½ tablespoons butter
2 cloves garlic, minced
3 shallots *or* 2 green onions, finely chopped
¼ pound mushrooms, finely processed
2 tablespoons chopped parsley
2 tablespoons Madeira, port, *or* lemon juice

Salt and freshly ground pepper to taste
6 veal scallops *or* turkey cutlets
Paprika
½ cup dry white wine
4 strips lemon rind, grated
4 green onions, thinly sliced

Preheat oven to 400°. Heat ½ tablespoon butter in a small heavy skillet. Add next 3 ingredients and sauté 3 minutes. Add parsley and Madeira; season to taste. Pound veal scallops until thin. Sprinkle with paprika. Place a heaping tablespoon of mushroom mixture on long end of each scallop. Roll up; secure tightly with string or toothpicks. Heat remaining 1 tablespoon butter in a large heavy skillet. Add veal rolls and sauté until lightly browned on all sides, about 4 minutes. Arrange veal rolls in an oven-proof dish. Add wine to skillet and deglaze the pan over high heat; pour over veal. Sprinkle with lemon rind and green onion. Cover dish tightly and bake for about 15 minutes.

Cream of Zucchini Soup with Crabmeat

Makes 4 servings

2½ tablespoons butter
1½ pounds zucchini, sliced
1 stalk celery, sliced
3 green onions, sliced
2 cups rich chicken broth
Bouquet garni (bay leaf, pinch of thyme, pinch of basil leaves, and a generous grinding of black pepper)

3 tablespoons flour
2 cans (13 ounces each) evaporated milk
¼ to ⅓ cup crabmeat
Shredded zucchini
Lemon slices

Melt ½ tablespoon butter in large heavy saucepan over medium heat. Add next 3 ingredients and cook, stirring occasionally, until vegetables are very tender, about 10 minutes. Add broth and bouquet garni. Increase heat and bring to a boil. Reduce heat and simmer 3 minutes. Melt remaining 2 tablespoons of butter in another large heavy saucepan over medium-low heat. Whisk in flour and cook, stirring, until bubbly. Add milk. Simmer 3 minutes, *do not boil.* Remove bay leaf from soup; process or blend until puréed. Combine purée with milk mixture. Refrigerate at least 2 hours or serve warm. Garnish with crabmeat, shredded zucchini, and lemon slices.

Green Beans Provencal

Makes 4 servings

1 teaspoon safflower oil *or* vegetable oil
2 to 3 tablespoons minced red onion
1 cup chopped tomatoes
1 clove garlic, minced
1 teaspoon paprika
½ teaspoon basil leaves

½ teaspoon thyme leaves
Grated rind of 1 orange
1 cup chicken broth *or* water
1 pound green beans, cut into 1½-inch pieces

Heat oil in medium saucepan. Add onion and sauté until softened, 3 to 5 minutes. Add remaining ingredients except green beans. Bring to a boil. Reduce heat; simmer, covered, 10 to 15 minutes. Add green beans. Cook, covered, until tender-crisp; about 5 minutes.

Variations

◆ **Mexican**: Omit paprika, basil, thyme, and orange rind. Add a dash of turmeric, cumin, and cilantro, 1 to 2 tablespoons hot salsa, and 1 teaspoon lemon *or* lime juice. Just before serving, sprinkle with 2 teaspoons chopped fresh cilantro *or* parsley.

◆ **Italian**: Omit paprika. Sprinkle with ¼ to ½ cup freshly grated Parmesan cheese. Toss to coat.

Braised Celery and Red Peppers

Makes 4 servings

8 stalks celery
4 teaspoons oil
1 onion, diced
½ cup diced red bell pepper

½ pound fresh mushrooms, sliced
Pinch thyme
Salt and pepper to taste

Cut celery stalks into 2-inch lengths. Blanch in boiling water for 5 minutes or until just tender. Drain, reserving ¼ cup liquid. Heat oil in a heavy skillet. Add onion, pepper, and mushrooms; sauté for 10 minutes. Add celery and ¼ cup liquid. Season with thyme, salt, and pepper. Cover and cook over low heat for 15 minutes.

Caviar and Olive Toast Rounds
Chicken in Red Pepper Butter
Casserole of Potatoes and Mushrooms
Miniature Vegetable Medley

Puréed red pepper means pizazz in this poultry menu. An easy, creamy Casserole of Potatoes and Mushrooms is a superb recipe to set off this spicy meat dish.

Casserole of Potatoes and Mushrooms
Makes 4 servings

1 pound baby new potatoes
½ pound fresh button mushrooms, trimmed
1 tablespoon butter
2 tablespoons flour
1 cup chicken broth

1 cup evaporated skim milk
Freshly ground pepper
Nutmeg to taste
Freshly minced parsley *or* freshly grated Parmesan cheese

Boil potatoes until just tender. Drain and set aside. Trim mushrooms and sauté in butter. Add flour and cook, stirring, until bubbly. Add liquids and stir until boiling. Stir in potatoes and simmer 10 minutes. Season with pepper and nutmeg, to taste. Transfer to serving dish and garnish with parsley or cheese.

Miniature Vegetable Medley
Makes 4 servings

¼ pound golden *or* red baby beets
¼ pound baby boiling onions
¼ pound baby carrots
¼ pound miniature zucchini

Boiling salted water plus 2 tablespoons lemon juice
Minced parsley
Freshly grated Romano cheese

Trim all vegetables. Peel beets, onions, and carrots; steam over lemon-water for 10 minutes. Add zucchini and steam another 5 to 8 minutes. Toss with parsley and Romano.

Chicken in Red Pepper Butter, Caviar and Olive Toast Rounds, page 60; Casserole of Potatoes and Mushrooms, Miniature Vegetable Medley, this page.

Caviar and Olive Toast Rounds

Makes 4 servings

¼ cup caviar
10 to 12 stuffed green olives, chopped
    fine
1 to 2 tablespoons minced red onion

2 to 3 tablespoons lemon juice
    Melba toast rounds
3 hard-boiled egg yolks, sieved

Mix first 4 ingredients. Spread on toast rounds and sprinkle with sieved yolks.

Chicken in Red Pepper Butter

Makes 4 servings

4 boned chicken breasts, halved
2 tablespoons butter
2 tablespoons vegetable oil

2 cloves garlic, minced
    Red Pepper Butter

Pound breasts to a thickness of ¼ inch. Heat butter, oil, and garlic in wide sauté pan. Sauté breasts, skin side down, over medium-high heat, 3 to 5 minutes per side. Transfer to platter and keep warm in oven. Serve breasts over Red Pepper Butter.

Red Pepper Butter

Makes approximately 3 cups

2 tablespoons butter
2 medium shallots, minced
2½ medium red bell peppers, sliced
3 tablespoons raspberry vinegar *or*
    red wine vinegar

¼ cup fresh lemon juice
½ cup dry white wine *or* vermouth
1 cup unsalted butter, melted

Melt 2 tablespoons butter in medium saucepan; sauté shallots and peppers. Stew over low heat, stirring often, until shallots and peppers are softened, about 8 minutes. Add vinegar and cook on high heat until reduced by two-thirds. Add lemon juice and wine. Reduce by half. Transfer to food processor and purée until smooth, 1 to 1½ minutes. Add 1 cup melted butter in thin stream while machine is running. Process 20 seconds longer. Just before serving, whisk sauce over low heat until hot to the touch. Do not simmer.

Note: Red Pepper Butter can be prepared 3 hours ahead of time. Cover and store at room temperature until serving time.

Cheddar Wafers with Apples
Mexican Snapper Verde
Steamed New Potatoes and Sesame Carrots
Green Salad with Mexican Dressing

Mexican Snapper Verde involves a unique blend of lime, cilantro, toasted almonds, and velvety avocado. It is just simply, not your standard fish dish; try it with whole snapper or trout. This salad completes the Mexican theme with a dressing comprised of authentic Mexican ingredients.

Cheddar Wafers with Apples
Makes 4 servings

1 cup flour
1¼ cups grated sharp Cheddar cheese
¼ pound butter
1 teaspoon Worcestershire sauce

Minced chives, cilantro, *or* parsley
Poppy, caraway, celery, *or* sesame seeds
Apple *or* pear wedges

Combine flour and cheese; cut in butter. Add sauce and blend well. Roll dough into long strips about ¾ inch in diameter. Freeze 15 minutes. Slice into thin wafers. Bake at 475° for 10 minutes on greased cookie sheet. Sprinkle wafers with different combinations of minced chives, cilantro, or parsley; poppy, caraway, celery, or sesame seeds. Serve with apple wedges.

Mexican Snapper Verde
Makes 4 servings

1½ pounds red snapper fillets
½ cup chopped cilantro *or* parsley
½ cup finely chopped toasted almonds
¼ cup butter

Lime juice
Salt and pepper to taste
Diced avocados

Place fish fillets in a baking dish. Sprinkle with cilantro and almonds. Melt butter in saucepan; add lime juice and season to taste. Pour over fish. Cover and bake at 350° for 30 minutes. Sprinkle with diced avocados and serve.

Steamed New Potatoes and Sesame Carrots

Makes 4 servings

10 to 12 small new potatoes
10 to 12 medium carrots
1 teaspoon butter
2 tablespoons sesame seeds
2 tablespoons butter

1 tablespoon honey
1 tablespoon grated orange rind
1 teaspoon grated gingerroot
Minced parsley

Scrub potatoes, but do not peel. Slice thinly and place in steamer. Peel and cut carrots into 3-inch sticks. Place in steamer above potatoes. Steam 15 minutes until tender. Melt 1 teaspoon butter in a medium skillet; add sesame seeds and toast until golden. Add the 2 tablespoons butter, honey, orange rind, and gingerroot; blend well. Remove carrots from steamer; toss in sesame glaze. Remove potatoes and sprinkle with parsley.

Green Salad with Mexican Dressing

Makes 4 servings

6 large radishes, sliced
1 large tomato, cut in wedges
4 to 6 large mushrooms, sliced
1 avocado, sliced
3 fresh peaches, sliced *or* 1 can (16 ounces) sliced Cling peaches, drained, optional

¼ head iceburg lettuce, torn into bite-sized pieces
¼ head romaine lettuce, torn into bite-sized pieces
Mexican Dressing
Shredded sharp Cheddar cheese

Arrange vegetables and fruit over lettuce in a large bowl. Add Mexican Dressing; toss and garnish with cheese. Serve immediately.

Mexican Dressing

Makes 1¼ cups

½ cup mild *or* hot taco sauce
¼ cup red wine vinegar
¼ cup salad oil
1 tablespoon minced parsley

1 tablespoon diced green chilies
1 teaspoon minced cilantro
1 teaspoon minced fresh oregano *or* ¼ teaspoon dried oregano

Combine all ingredients; mix thoroughly. Serve as directed.

Mexican Snapper Verde (Cod Variation), page 61;
Steamed New Potatoes and Sesame Carrots, Green
Salad with Mexican Dressing, this page.

> Ceviche
> Chicken in Nut Sauce
> Mexican Garlic Bread
> Creamed Spinach
> Tomato Cucumber Vinaigrette

*Ceviche is traditionally an appetizer for the seafood gourmet;
here is a Fast and Fresh variation for you. It is lovely when
presented on little scallop shells with thin twists of lemon.
The Tomato Cucumber Vinaigrette demonstrates
how a properly composed salad can lend
an attractive aire of expertise to your menu.*

Ceviche

Makes 4 servings

1 pound cooked fish (mixture of bay shrimp, scallops, and squid *or* white fish fillets, cubed)
1 California avocado, diced
2 green onions, minced
6 to 8 cherry tomatoes, halved
¼ cup lime juice
¼ cup salsa

1 teaspoon oil
1 teaspoon white *or* red wine vinegar
¼ teaspoon oregano leaves
1 to 2 tablespoons sliced jalapeno peppers *or* diced green chilies
1 to 2 tablespoons chopped cilantro
Scallop shells, optional
Lemon twists, optional

Marinate fish and avocados in a mixture of onions, tomatoes, lime juice, salsa, oil, vinegar, and oregano in refrigerator at least one hour or overnight. Drain and toss with peppers and cilantro. Chill before serving. Serve in scallop shells with lemon twists, if desired.

Mexican Garlic Bread

Makes 4 servings

3 to 4 sourdough *or* sweet French rolls
½ cup butter, softened
½ cup mozzarella cheese, shredded
2 cloves garlic, minced

¼ cup minced cilantro
½ teaspoon chili powder
¼ teaspoon cumin

Preheat broiler. Cut rolls in half. Mix remaining ingredients and spread on cut sides of rolls. Broil until topping is golden and bubbly, 2 to 3 minutes.

Chicken in Nut Sauce

Makes 4 servings

1 tablespoon safflower oil *or* vegetable oil
2 boned chicken breasts, halved
½ pound potatoes, peeled
1 jar (12 ounces) chili sauce
¼ cup salsa
½ cup chicken broth

1 package (2½ ounces) almonds, finely chopped
Garnishes:
Whole almonds, roughly chopped
Cilantro, finely chopped
Ripe olives, sliced
Sour cream

Heat oil in a roasting pan; brown chicken and potatoes. Combine the next 4 ingredients in a medium saucepan and bring to a boil. Pour mixture over chicken and potatoes. Cover and bake at 375° for 30 to 45 minutes, until potatoes are done and chicken is tender. Garnish with a sprinkling of almonds, cilantro, olives, and sour cream.

Creamed Spinach

Makes 4 servings

1 tablespoon butter
2 bunches spinach leaves, chopped *or* kale, *or* chard
2 tablespoons water
1 package (3 ounces) cream cheese, softened

⅛ teaspoon nutmeg
Salt to taste
Freshly ground pepper to taste

Melt butter in a large frying pan over medium-high heat. Add spinach, water, and cream cheese. Cover and cook 5 minutes, or until spinach is tender. Add seasonings and mix well.

Tomato Cucumber Vinaigrette

Makes 4 servings

1 bunch watercress leaves
4 medium tomatoes, sliced
½ cucumber, thinly sliced

1 small red *or* yellow onion, separated into rings
Vinaigrette

Line plates with watercress. Alternate with rings of tomato and cucumber. Top with onion rings. Garnish center with more watercress. Pour Vinaigrette over salad.

Vinaigrette

Makes 1 cup

¼ cup olive oil *or* nut flavored oil *or* vegetable oil
2 tablespoons lemon *or* lime juice
1 teaspoon Dijon-style mustard

1 teaspoon minced fresh tarragon *or* ¼ teaspoon dried tarragon
1 teaspoon minced fresh thyme *or* ¼ teaspoon dried thyme

Combine all ingredients; mix well.

Cracked Crab Legs
Nut-Studded Turkey Tenderloins in
Tangerine Beurre Blanc
Poppy Seed Noodles
Fluted Major Mushrooms
Tomato and Golden Squash Sauté

Rolling turkey tenderloins in ground nuts, results in a stylishly different, as well as tasty, presentation. This entrée also calls for a simple pasta to share the tempting Tangerine Beurre Blanc.

Nut-Studded Turkey Tenderloins in Tangerine Beurre Blanc

Makes 4 servings

½ cup ground toasted almonds *or* pistachios
1 to 2 tablespoons grated tangerine rind
1¼ pounds turkey tenderloins *or* breasts, pounded ½ inch thick

1 tablespoon butter
2 to 3 cloves garlic, minced
Tangerine Beurre Blanc
Tangerine slices, optional

Mix nuts with tangerine rind. Moisten tenderloins with water; then bread with nut mixture. Melt butter in medium skillet and sauté tenderloins and garlic for 5 minutes on each side. Serve tenderloins over Tangerine Beurre Blanc. Garnish with tangerine slices, if desired.

Tangerine Beurre Blanc

3 tangerines, peeled and chopped
1 tablespoon grated tangerine rind
½ cup dry white wine

¼ cup lemon *or* lime juice
½ pound unsalted butter, melted

Cook tangerines and rind in wine and lemon juice; reduce by half. Transfer to a food processor and purée until smooth. Add butter in thin stream while machine is running. Process 20 seconds longer. Just before serving, whisk sauce over low heat until just hot to the touch. Do not simmer.

Note: Tangerine Beurre Blanc can be prepared up to 3 hours in advance. Cover and store at room temperature until serving time.

Poppy Seed Noodles, Fluted Major Mushrooms, Tomato and Golden Squash Sauté, Cracked Crab Legs, page 68; Nut-Studded Turkey Tenderloins in Tangerine Beurre Blanc, this page.

Cracked Crab Legs

Makes 4 servings

4 crab legs, boiled and cracked
Lemon juice *or* lime juice

Tangerine rind

Sprinkle crab legs with lemon juice and tangerine rind. Serve with seafood forks.
Note: Cracked Crab Legs can also be served with the Tangerine Beurre Blanc to give guests a preview of the entrée.

Poppy Seed Noodles

Makes 4 servings

2 quarts water
½ teaspoon salt
8 ounces medium noodles
1 tablespoon safflower oil *or*
    vegetable oil

1 to 2 tablespoons butter, optional
1 to 2 tablespoons lemon juice, optional
1 to 2 teaspoons poppy seeds

Bring water and salt to a boil. Add noodles and oil; cook, uncovered, until tender but firm, 5 to 8 minutes. Drain; add butter and lemon juice, if desired. Toss noodles gently with poppy seeds to mix.

Fluted Major Mushrooms

Makes 4 servings

4 major, giant mushrooms
1 tablespoon butter

1 teaspoon lemon juice

Trim and flute mushrooms. Melt butter in medium skillet. Sauté mushrooms, cap side down, over medium-high heat. Turn once, and sauté until golden. Sprinkle with lemon juice.

Tomato and Golden Squash Sauté

Makes 4 servings

2 yellow crookneck squash
2 tablespoons safflower oil *or*
    vegetable oil
1 to 2 large cloves garlic, minced

12 cherry tomatoes
½ teaspoon basil *or* thyme
Salt and freshly ground pepper to taste

Trim ends from squash and quarter lengthwise. Cut crosswise in ½-inch thick slices. Heat oil in a large skillet. Sauté squash and garlic over medium-high heat until squash starts to brown, about 5 minutes. Add tomatoes and basil; continue to sauté until tomatoes are just warm, 2 to 4 minutes. Season to taste with salt and pepper.

> Mussels in Herb Butter
> Rosemary Cream Chicken
> Rosemary Loaf
> Sautéed Savoy Cabbage
> Tomato and Cheese Salad

Chicken becomes special when it is simmered in a fragrant rosemary cream sauce spiked with a little Dijon-style mustard. Warm slices of Rosemary Loaf become the natural accompaniment.

Mussels in Herb Butter

Makes 4 servings

2 dozen fresh mussels *or* frozen mussels
½ cup softened butter
2 tablespoons chopped parsley
1 tablespoon lemon juice

1 shallot, minced
3 large cloves garlic, minced
1 slice cooked bacon, crumbled
Freshly ground pepper

Steam well-scrubbed and debearded mussels until they open. Save a half-shell for each mussel. Blend the remaining ingredients thoroughly. Put a small amount of herbed butter in each shell. Lay mussel on it. Cover with more butter and arrange them in a single layer in shallow baking pans. Heat oven to 450° and bake for 10 to 15 minutes. Serve sizzling, on cocktail plates with seafood forks or on a tray with toothpicks.

Tomato and Cheese Salad

Makes 4 servings

2 tomatoes, sliced
1 medium red onion, thinly sliced
1 cucumber, thinly sliced
½ pound mozzarella cheese, shredded

Juice of 1 lemon
2 to 3 tablespoons olive oil *or* vegetable oil
Salt and freshly ground pepper

Top tomatoes with onion and cucumber slices. Combine cheese, lemon juice, and oil; season to taste. Pour dressing over tomatoes.

Rosemary Cream Chicken

Makes 4 servings

4 boned chicken breasts, halved,
   skinned, and pounded
½ cup flour
1 tablespoon minced fresh rosemary
   leaves
2 to 3 cloves garlic, minced
1 tablespoon butter
1 tablespoon oil

½ cup whipping cream
½ cup half-and-half
2 teaspoons Dijon-style mustard
¾ cup sliced mushrooms
½ cup shredded Swiss cheese
2 to 3 tablespoons minced green chives
   or onion

Coat chicken in a mixture of flour and rosemary. Heat garlic, butter, and oil over medium-high heat. Sauté breasts until golden, 3 minutes per side. Do not crowd pan. Add next four ingredients. Simmer 5 to 8 minutes. Remove chicken; boil to reduce sauce. Just before serving, stir in cheese and sprinkle with chives.

Rosemary Loaf

Makes 4 servings

1 round (1 pound) French *or*
   Italian Loaf, sliced
½ cup butter, softened
1 tablespoon chopped fresh *or*
   1 teaspoon dried rosemary, crushed

2 to 3 tablespoons minced fresh parsley
1 teaspoon lemon juice
¼ cup grated Romano *or* Parmesan
   cheese

Preheat broiler. Slice bread. Combine remaining ingredients thoroughly, spread evenly over slices. Broil until cheese is bubbly and golden brown.

Sautéed Savoy Cabbage

Makes 4 servings

1 tablespoon butter
1 medium Savoy *or* green cabbage,
   trimmed and cut crosswise into ½-inch
   strips

½ cup coarsely chopped canned water
   chestnuts
1 tablespoon honey
1 teaspoon salt

Melt butter in a large skillet over medium-high heat. Add cabbage and sauté, tossing often, about 4 minutes. Stir in remaining ingredients. Sauté, tossing occasionally, until tender-crisp, 4 to 6 minutes.

Tomato and Cheese Salad, Mussels in Herb Butter,
page 69; Rosemary Cream Chicken, Rosemary Loaf,
Sautéed Savoy Cabbage, this page.

> **Boursin and Red Grapes**
> **Lemon-Lime Breaded Tenderloins**
> **Wild Rice Pilaf**
> **Butter-Steamed Leeks**
> **Iced Tomato Soup**

*Presentation is prime in this menu. It begins with a beautiful
array of Boursin and Red Grapes. The entrée is brightly
garnished with citrus fruits and avocados.
For additional color dramatics, serve
the savory sipping soup in tall, chilled flutes.*

Butter-Steamed Leeks

Makes 4 servings

1 bunch leeks
1 tablespoon butter
¼ cup water

¼ cup freshly grated Romano *or*
Parmesan cheese

Trim leek root ends and remove most of green leaves. Split lengthwise and wash under cold water, separating leaves to clean thoroughly. Melt butter in a wide frying pan over medium-high heat until it browns slightly. Add leeks and water. Cover; increase heat to high, and cook until tender, 3 to 5 minutes. Sprinkle with cheese before serving.

Iced Tomato Soup

Makes 4 servings

1 cup plain yogurt
1 cup cream cheese, softened
1 cup milk
3 cups tomato juice
1 tablespoon grated red onion
2 teaspoons lemon juice

¼ teaspoon salt
Dash Tabasco sauce
1 to 2 tablespoons finely chopped mint
Freshly ground pepper
½ cucumber, peeled, seeded, and diced
Mint sprigs

Combine yogurt and cheese in a food processor; process briefly. Add next seven ingredients and process. Taste and season with freshly ground pepper. Cover and chill thoroughly. Serve garnished with diced cucumber and mint sprigs.

Boursin and Red Grapes

Makes 4 servings

¼ cup Boursin *or* other cream cheese
½ teaspoon evaporated skim milk
20 large, seedless flame red *or* green
grapes

⅓ cup minced pistachios, toasted

With an electric mixer, whip cheese and milk until smooth and fluffy. Pat about ½ teaspoon of cheese around each grape. Place coated grapes on a flat pan in a single layer and freeze until firm, 10 to 15 minutes. Roll grapes in pistachios. Gently cut grapes in half with a sharp knife. Arrange cut side up on a tray.

Note: Boursin and Red Grapes may be prepared 3 hours in advance. Store in refrigerator until serving time.

Lemon-Lime Breaded Tenderloins

Makes 4 servings

4 turkey tenderloins *or* chicken breasts, skinned
1 egg
2 tablespoons water
½ cup seasoned bread crumbs
2 tablespoons grated orange rind
2 tablespoons grated lemon rind

½ cup flour
2 tablespoons butter
2 tablespoons vegetable oil
Sliced avocado
Sliced orange, grapefruit, *or* kiwi fruit
Lemon twists

Preheat oven to 200°. Pound tenderloins to a thickness of ¼ inch. Combine egg and water; beat lightly. Blend crumbs and citrus rinds. Coat turkey first with flour, then with egg mixture, and last with crumb mixture. Heat butter and oil in a wide frying pan and sauté the tenderloins until golden brown, 3 to 5 minutes per side. Do not crowd pan. Garnish with fruit of your choice and lemon twists.

Wild Rice Pilaf

Makes 4 servings

1 tablespoon butter
2 to 3 cloves garlic, minced
1 cup wild rice
2 cups chicken broth
2 cups water
¼ cup chopped yellow *or* green onion

¼ cup chopped mushrooms
¼ cup chopped celery
2 to 3 tablespoons minced parsley
2 tablespoons chopped pimiento, optional
Salt and freshly ground pepper to taste

Melt butter in large skillet over medium-high heat. Sauté garlic and rice for 3 minutes. Add broth and bring to a boil. Reduce heat and simmer, covered, 45 minutes. Stir in remaining ingredients. Cook until warmed through.

Note: Chopped green, yellow, purple, or red pepper and grated carrot make colorful variations on this basic pilaf.

Spinach Cress Dip with Vegetables and Fruit
Gourmet Seafood Pizza
Green Leaf and Cilantro Salad

Pizza like this is quite presentable for guests. The cheese is in the crust, as well as in the topping. This entire bill of fare is designed for fun, flavor, and flair — essential elements for casual entertaining.

Spinach Cress Dip with Vegetables and Fruit
Makes 1½ cups

½ bunch watercress, roughly chopped
½ bunch spinach, roughly chopped
2 fillets *or* anchovies *or* 2 tablespoons lime *or* lemon juice
2 tablespoons minced parsley

¼ teaspoon tarragon leaves
1 clove garlic, minced
1 cup mayonnaise
Assorted raw vegetables and fruits

Combine all ingredients, except vegetables and fruits, in a blender or food processor. Process until smooth. Serve with assorted raw vegetables and fruits, prepared in bite-sized pieces.

Green Leaf and Cilantro Salad
Makes 4 servings

1 head butter lettuce, torn
1 head red leaf lettuce, torn
½ jicama or daikon, coarsely shredded
1 bunch cilantro, stems removed

½ cup mild salsa
¼ cup safflower oil *or* vegetable oil
3 tablespoons raspberry vinegar *or* red wine vinegar

Mix lettuce, jicama, and cilantro. Combine remaining ingredients; mix well. Pour over salad and toss.

Gourmet Seafood Pizza, page 76; Spinach Cress Dip with Vegetables and Fruit, Green Leaf and Cilantro Salad, this page.

Gourmet Seafood Pizza

Makes 4 servings

1 package dry yeast
⅔ cup very warm water
2 tablespoons butter, melted
½ to 1 teaspoon sugar *or* fructose
1 cup whole wheat flour
1 cup all-purpose flour
1½ cups shredded mozzarella cheese
½ cup grated Parmesan cheese
¼ teaspoon salt

1 cup tomato sauce
1½ ounces mozzarella cheese, shredded
½ ounce Parmesan cheese, grated
2 ounces shrimp
2 ounces scallops
8 tomato halves
Chopped fresh basil
8 avocado crescents

Dissolve yeast in water. Stir in butter and sugar until frothy. Combine flour, cheese, and salt in a mixer or food processor. Add yeast mixture and process with a few on/off turns until well blended. Add more flour, as needed, to achieve a sticky, but not wet, texture. Let machine run 40 seconds to knead dough. Cover and set in a warm place to rise.

Punch down and line a pizza pan with dough. Spread with tomato sauce. Sprinkle with cheese and seafood. Arrange tomato halves in pinwheel fashion. Bake in a 425° oven for 8 to 10 minutes. Garnish with a sprinkling of basil and a pinwheel of avocado crescents.

Note: Recommended cooking time is for a thick crust pizza, using a 12-inch deep-dish pizza pan. A larger pan *or* cookie sheet may be used if a thin crust is desired; adjust cooking time accordingly.

Pizza Topping Variations

◆ **Mexican Sausage:** Omit shredded mozzarella and Parmesan, shrimp, scallops, basil, and avocados. Top with ¼ pound browned ground *or* sliced sausage, ½ cup diced green peppers, ½ cup chopped onions, and ¼ cup sliced olives. Sprinkle with 1 cup shredded Cheddar cheese and chili powder to taste. Bake as directed. Serve with sour cream, if desired.

◆ **Oriental Turkey:** Omit shrimp, scallops, basil, and avocados. Top with 1 cup cooked turkey, ¼ cup sliced water chestnuts, and ¼ cup bean sprouts. Sprinkle with coriander and ginger to taste. Bake as directed. Serve with soy sauce and plain yogurt, if desired.

Skewered Scallops
Steak Sauté Cognac
Pommes a la Parisienne
Golden Vegetable Soup
Baby Green Peas with Lettuce
Celery Root Remoulade

*Don't overlook this flash-in-the-pan technique
of preparing spectacular steaks or the opportunity
to impress your guests with this flaming presentation.
They'll also be enchanted by the Pommes Parisienne
and the Baby Green Peas with Lettuce.*

Steak Sauté Cognac

Makes 4 servings

1 teaspoon butter
1 teaspoon safflower oil *or* vegetable oil
1½ pounds top round, sirloin,
   or flank steak

¼ cup brandy
Minced fresh parsley, optional

Heat butter and oil in a large skillet over medium-high heat. Brown steak well on both sides, 3 to 5 minutes per side for rare. Add brandy. Heat and ignite, shaking until flame dies. Remove meat to carving board. Sprinkle with minced parsley, if desired.

Steak au Poivre Variation

2 tablespoons black peppercorns
2 tablespoons butter

2 tablespoons lemon juice
Dash Worcestershire sauce

Before sautéing meat, crush two tablespoons black peppercorns. Press peppercorns firmly into both sides of steak. In a saucepan over medium heat, melt butter in lemon juice. Stir in a dash of Worcestershire sauce. Pour over flambéed steaks.

Roast Cognac Variation

1 tablespoon butter
2 teaspoons vegetable oil
1½ to 2 pounds sirloin tip roast

½ cup brandy
Minced fresh parsley

Brown roast as directed. Bake in a 150° oven 45 minutes for rare. Flambé with brandy. Transfer to carving board and sprinkle with parsley, if desired.

Skewered Scallops

Makes 4 servings

1 pound medium sea scallops
1 pint cherry tomatoes
2 medium green peppers, cut into
1-inch squares
⅓ cup lemon juice

3 tablespoons honey
3 tablespoons Dijon-style mustard
2 tablespoons safflower oil *or*
vegetable oil
1½ teaspoons curry

Alternate scallops, tomatoes, and green peppers on toothpicks approximately 3 inches long. Place on broiler pan. Combine remaining ingredients. Brush skewers with sauce. Broil about 4 inches from heat source for 5 to 7 minutes. Turn carefully; brush with sauce. Broil 5 to 7 minutes longer, basting once.

Golden Vegetable Soup

Makes 4 servings

1 teaspoon butter
1 small red onion, chopped
1 leek, sliced (white part only)
3 cups rich broth *or* 1½ cans (14 ounces
each) low-sodium chicken broth
1 small potato, diced

1 small turnip, diced
8 small carrots, sliced
¼ to ½ teaspoon thyme *or* basil leaves
Salt to taste
Freshly ground pepper to taste
½ cup Neufchatel, kefir, *or* plain yogurt

Melt butter in 3 or 4-quart saucepan. Add onion and leek; cook, stirring, until softened and translucent. Add remaining ingredients, except cheese. Bring broth to a boil, reduce heat, cover, and simmer about 20 minutes or until vegetables are softened. In a blender or food processor, whirl soup until smooth. Return to pan and season to taste. Heat to simmering or chill and serve cold. Garnish each serving with Neufchatel, kefir, or yogurt.

Baby Green Peas with Lettuce

Makes 4 servings

1 tablespoon butter
10 ounces frozen baby peas
2 cups packed, finely shredded lettuce
1 tablespoon chopped fresh basil *or*
mint, *or* 1 teaspoon dried basil *or* mint
leaves

2 tablespoons minced parsley
Salt to taste
Sugar to taste
Nutmeg to taste

Melt butter in a large frying pan over medium heat. Add peas. Cover and cook until thawed, about 5 minutes. Add lettuce, basil, and parsley. Cook, uncovered, until lettuce wilts. Toss occasionally. Season to taste and serve.

*Steak Sauté Cognac (Roast Cognac Variation),
page 77; Pommes a la Parisienne, page 80; Skewered
Scallops, Baby Green Peas with Lettuce, Golden
Vegetable Soup, this page.*

Pommes a la Parisienne

Makes 4 servings

16 small new red potatoes
1 tablespoon butter

3 tablespoons chopped parsley, dill,
  or chives

Peel a thin strip of skin from around the middle of each potato. Place potatoes in a saucepan; cover with water. Bring to a boil, reduce heat, and simmer, covered, until tender, about 25 minutes. Drain. Melt butter in a saucepan over low heat; add potatoes. Shake pan gently until potatoes are well coated with butter. Sprinkle with parsley, dill, or chives.

Mexicali Spicy Variation

1 tablespoon oil
½ teaspoon ground turmeric
1 diced green chili *or* jalapeno pepper

¼ teaspoon cumin *or* chili powder
1 tablespoon freshly chopped cilantro
  or parsley

Prepare potatoes as directed above. In oil, sauté turmeric, green chili, and cumin. Add drained potatoes and shake pan gently until they are well coated. Sprinkle with cilantro or parsley.

Celery Root Remoulade

Makes 4 servings

2 tablespoons lemon juice
2 celery roots
¼ cup Neufchatel cheese
¼ cup plain yogurt
1 egg yolk
1 to 2 teaspoons Dijon-style mustard
2 teaspoons drained capers, finely
  chopped, optional

2 green onions, thinly sliced
1 clove garlic, minced
1 teaspoon lemon juice
¼ teaspoon thyme leaves
2 tablespoons finely chopped fresh
  parsley *or* chives
  Butter lettuce leaves

In a large bowl, combine 8 cups of cold water and 2 tablespoons lemon juice. Peel celery roots and shred them coarsely. Add to lemon water, mix well, and let stand about 5 minutes. Drain well. In a medium bowl, blend Neufchatel and yogurt. Beat in next 7 ingredients. Add drained celery root, tossing lightly until coated with dressing. Cover and refrigerate until chilled. Sprinkle with parsley and serve on butter lettuce leaves.

Mozzarella Mexicana
Spicy Beef Brochettes
Cumin Corn on the Cob
Green Bean or Cauliflower Purée
Sopa De Tortilla

Contrasting textures result in casual entertaining fare. Corn on the cob is an on-going favorite enhanced with snappy cumin; and the Sopa De Tortilla, with its myriad of colorful garnishes, lends pizazz to this popular Mexican theme.

Sopa De Tortilla

Makes 4 servings

4 corn tortillas, cut into ¼-inch strips
  Vegetable oil
⅓ cup red onion, finely chopped
2 cloves garlic, minced
1 teaspoon butter
1 can (16 ounces) tomatillos,
  drained and crushed
1 jar (12 ounces) chili dip
3 cups chicken broth

Olives, sliced
Cilantro sprigs *or* parsley sprigs
Monterey Jack cheese, shredded
Cheddar cheese, shredded
Radishes, sliced
Sour cream, optional
Lime wedges
Avocados, diced

Fry tortilla strips in hot oil until hardened but not browned. Drain on paper towels and set aside. Sauté onion and garlic in butter until softened. Add crushed tomatillos, chili dip, and broth. Bring to boiling. Reduce heat and simmer, about 10 minutes. To serve, place tortilla strips in bottom of bowl, and ladle in soup. Garnish from selection of remaining ingredients.

Cumin Corn on the Cob

Makes 4 servings

6 ears fresh young corn, boiled and
  drained
2 limes, cut in wedges

½ cup butter, softened
1 teaspoon cumin
½ teaspoon cayenne

Arrange corn ears on a serving platter and garnish with lime wedges. Combine butter, cumin, and cayenne; mix well and serve with hot corn.

Mozzarella Mexicana

Makes 4 servings

1 brick mozzarella *or* low-fat Farmers
   cheese *or* Mexican white cheese
1 cup non-fat milk
1 cup flour

1 cup fine bread crumbs
   Safflower oil *or* vegetable oil
½ cup taco sauce

Cut cheese into ½-inch thick rectangular slices. Dip cheese into milk and coat with flour; dip into milk again, and roll in bread crumbs. Heat oil ¼ inch deep in a heavy skillet. Place slices of cheese in hot oil. Cook until browned on one side. Turn and brown other side. Do not overcook or cheese will melt into oil. Remove cheese and arrange on a glass serving plate. Serve with taco sauce.

Spicy Beef Brochettes

Makes 4 servings

1 pound beef, lamb, chicken *or* turkey
   breast, cubed
1¾ cups taco sauce
¼ cup beef *or* chicken broth
¼ cup red wine vinegar
8 cherry tomatoes
4 mushrooms, halved

8 zucchini slices
8 cubes yellow crookneck squash
8 boiling *or* button onions
½ green pepper, cut in squares
½ red pepper, cut in squares
2 to 3 tablespoons olive oil *or*
   safflower oil

Marinate meat in 1 cup taco sauce, broth, and vinegar overnight. Secure meat and vegetables on skewers. Bake in 400° oven for 15 to 20 minutes, or until medium-rare. Combine remaining ¾ cup taco sauce and oil; mix well. Pour over kebabs, or serve on the side.

Green Bean or Cauliflower Purée

Makes 4 servings

1½ pounds young green beans, cut into
   1-inch lengths *or* 1½ to 2 pounds
   cauliflower

1 teaspoon butter
   Salt and freshly ground pepper to taste
   Nutmeg (for cauliflower)

Plunge beans into a large kettle of boiling water and boil, uncovered, for 10 to 15 minutes. Beans need to be well-cooked so they can be blended to a smooth purée. Drain beans in a colander, reserving some liquid. Process or blend beans a portion at a time, adding a little of the cooking liquid if needed. Reheat the purée with butter in a saucepan. Add salt and pepper to taste. Keep purée warm over hot water if not served immediately.

If cauliflower is used, break into florets and cook in boiling water until soft, about 15 minutes. Process and reheat as described for beans. Season with salt, pepper, and nutmeg to taste.

Cumin Corn on the Cob, Sopa De Tortilla, page 81;
Spicy Beef Brochettes, Green Bean or Cauliflower
Purée, Mozzarella Mexicana, this page.
Overleaf: *Citrus Salad with Yogurt Dressing,*
Golden Cauliflower, page 86; Greek Lamb Stir-Fry,
Pine Nut Pilaf, Vegetable Herbed Cheese, page 87.

> Vegetable Herbed Cheese
> Greek Lamb Stir-Fry
> Pine Nut Pilaf
> Golden Cauliflower
> Citrus Salad with
> Yogurt Orange Dressing

*Your guests will be intrigued by the blend of flavors in this
easy make-ahead appetizer. They'll find this Greek version
of the Oriental stir-fry incredibly clever, and
the Pine Nut Pilaf will be utterly irresistable.*

Golden Cauliflower
Makes 4 servings

2 tablespoons butter
4 cups thinly sliced cauliflower
⅓ cup water

1 cup shredded Cheddar cheese
1 teaspoon paprika

Melt butter in large skillet; add cauliflower and water. Cover and steam over high heat for 3 minutes. Sprinkle with cheese and paprika; cover and continue steaming until cheese melts and cauliflower is tender, about 2 minutes.

Citrus Salad with Yogurt Orange Dressing
Makes 4 servings

2 small heads butter *or* Bibb lettuce
1 avocado, sliced

1 orange, sliced
Yogurt Orange Dressing

Separate lettuce into leaves. Top with avocado, orange slices and Yogurt Orange Dressing.

Yogurt Orange Dressing
Makes 1¼ cups

1 cup plain yogurt
¼ cup orange juice
2 teaspoons grated orange rind

Powdered sugar to taste
Dash ground cloves

Mix all ingredients and let stand to blend flavors.

Vegetable Herbed Cheese

Makes 4 servings

1 package (8 ounces) Neufchatel cheese, softened
1 carrot, grated
1 stalk celery, finely chopped
1 tablespoon lemon juice
2 tablespoons minced fresh parsley
1 clove garlic, minced

1 teaspoon fresh basil leaves, chopped or ¼ teaspoon basil
1 teaspoon fresh thyme leaves, chopped or ¼ teaspoon thyme
1 teaspoon fresh oregano leaves, chopped or ¼ teaspoon oregano
Fresh ground pepper

Blend all ingredients thoroughly. Mound into a small glass bowl or press into a lightly oiled mold. Cover and chill well before serving.

Greek Lamb Stir-Fry

Makes 4 servings

1 tablespoon olive oil or vegetable oil
1 pound lamb, cubed (shoulder, shank, or leg)
⅓ cup pine nuts
1 red onion, diced
2 to 3 cloves garlic, minced
1 cup red wine
1 cup beef broth
¼ cup minced fresh parsley

1 to 2 teaspoons chopped fresh mint or parsley
1 teaspoon oregano
1 small eggplant, diced or 1 cup broccoli florets
1 teaspoon arrowroot, optional
Sliced olives
Parsley or mint

Heat oil in a wok or skillet. Add lamb, pine nuts, onion, and garlic; sauté until lamb is browned and pine nuts are golden. Deglaze wok with wine. Add broth, parsley, mint, and oregano; simmer about 25 minutes. Add eggplant during the last 10 minutes of cooking time. Reduce liquid over high heat or thicken by stirring in arrowroot, if desired. Garnish with olives and sprinkle with parsley.

Pine Nut Pilaf

Makes 4 servings

1 tablespoon olive oil or vegetable oil
1 medium red onion, minced
2 to 3 garlic cloves, minced
1¼ cups long-grain rice
⅓ cup pine nuts or slivered almonds

2¼ cups chicken broth
¼ cup lemon juice
1 to 2 tablespoons chopped fresh mint
Freshly grated rind of 1 lemon
Freshly ground pepper

Heat oil in a medium saucepan over medium-high heat. Add onion and cloves; sauté until soft, about 5 minutes. Add rice and nuts; stir until golden brown. Add broth and lemon juice; bring to a boil. Reduce heat; cover and simmer until liquid is absorbed, 20 to 25 minutes. Just before serving, add mint, lemon rind, and pepper; fluff with two forks.

Greek Salad
Broiled Beef on Basil Tomato Sauce
Spaghetti Squash
Fresh Artichoke Halves
Whole Wheat Herb Biscuits

This bright red Basil Tomato Sauce is a beautiful backdrop
for a Broiled Beef menu. Green and gold vegetables
dramatize the color and flavor of the entrée; but the best
thing about this menu, is the fast and fresh theme that runs
throughout, right down to the quick biscuits.

Broiled Beef on Basil Tomato Sauce

Makes 4 servings

1 tablespoon safflower oil
1 clove garlic, minced
2 green onions, minced
1½ cups Bordeaux Sauce (page 95)
¼ pound tomatoes, peeled, seeded, and diced

1 to 2 tablespoons tomato paste
¼ cup chopped fresh basil
1½ pounds beef eye *or* round steak, thinly sliced

Heat oil in a skillet; sauté garlic and onions, until soft, about 3 minutes. Add Bordeaux Sauce and tomatoes. Cook over medium heat 15 minutes. Thicken and color with tomato paste. Just before serving, stir in basil. Broil beef and serve on a bed of Basil Tomato Sauce.

Spaghetti Squash

Makes 4 servings

1 spaghetti squash, quartered   Freshly grated Parmesan cheese

Cover squash with water and cook over medium-high heat for 20 minutes or until tender. Drain. Remove and shred pulp with fork. Top with Parmesan cheese.

Fresh Artichoke Halves

Makes 4 servings

4 artichokes
2 lemons

¼ cup chopped fresh parsley
Freshly ground black pepper

Trim tough bottom leaves off artichokes; cut off tips of remaining leaves with scissors; remove stems. Rub all exposed cut surfaces with a lemon half. Fill a large pot with water to a depth of 1 inch. Add juice of ½ lemon. Bring to a boil. Arrange artichokes in the pot, stem side up. Place a wet towel over the top of the pot. Cover and cook over medium heat until artichokes are tender, 30 to 45 minutes. Cut each in half. Serve with sliced lemon, parsley, and pepper.

Whole Wheat Herb Biscuits

Makes 1 dozen

1½ cups whole wheat flour
¼ cup wheat germ
¼ cup all-purpose flour
2½ teaspoons baking powder
1 teaspoon salt
1 tablespoon sugar

1 tablespoon chopped basil
1 tablespoon chopped chives
1 tablespoon chopped parsley
⅛ to ¼ cup butter, sliced
¾ cup low-fat milk

Combine first 9 ingredients in a food processor. Process briefly to combine. Add butter and process with several on/off turns until the consistency of coarse corn meal. While processor is running, pour in milk; process until just moistened. Turn dough onto a lightly floured surface. Knead lightly for 30 seconds. Pat to a thickness of ½ inch. Cut with a biscuit cutter. Bake for 10 to 12 minutes in a 450° oven.

Greek Salad

Makes 4 servings

1 head red lettuce, roughly chopped
2 green onions, chopped
1 small cucumber, quartered and sliced
3 ounces feta cheese, crumbled
Greek olives

¼ cup olive oil
3 tablespoons red wine vinegar
Dash dry mustard
Cherry tomatoes, optional

Combine lettuce, onions, cucumber, cheese, and olives; toss gently. Whisk together oil, vinegar, and mustard. Pour over salad and toss. Garnish with cherry tomatoes, if desired.

Smoked Salmon a la Russe
Poached Chicken Breasts and Vermicelli in Wine
Brussels Sprouts and Creamed Carrots
Sherried Escarole Salad

*Poaching poultry achieves a moist and succulent entrée —
the dish simmers on its own — no need to hover over the sauté
pan. Use this free time to give extra attention to the dainty
Creamed Carrot flowers that turn these
Brussels sprouts into a detailed work of art.*

Smoked Salmon a la Russe
Makes 4 servings

1 thin loaf French bread, sliced
  Sour cream
2 packages (4 ounces each) smoked
  salmon, thinly sliced
4 ounces caviar

Butter lettuce cups
Capers
Tomato wedges
Lemon twists

Spread bread slices with sour cream. Shape salmon slices into coronets; spoon a little caviar into each coronet. Place coronets on bread slices and arrange on lettuce cups. Garnish with remaining ingredients.

Sherried Escarole Salad
Makes 4 servings

12 medium *or* 8 large mushrooms,
  trimmed
2 heads escarole *or* endive, torn
2 green onions, chopped

½ cup plain yogurt
1½ teaspoons Dijon-style mustard
1 to 2 tablespoons dry sherry

Arrange mushrooms on escarole. Mix together remaining ingredients and spoon half of dressing over salad. Serve balance of dressing on the side.

*Braised Celery Almondine, Gingered Chicken with
Apples, Fruited Watercress Salad, page 20;
Whole Wheat Macaroni (Colored Pasta Variation),
Vegetable Fromage, page 18.*

Poached Chicken Breasts and Vermicelli in Wine

Makes 4 servings

1 teaspoon butter
1 teaspoon oil
½ pound mushrooms, sliced
4 boned chicken breasts, skinned and
   halved
¼ teaspoon salt

½ teaspoon tarragon
⅛ teaspoon pepper
2 tablespoons minced fresh parsley
¾ cup dry white wine
1 teaspoon arrowroot, optional
8 ounces vermicelli, cooked and drained

Melt butter and oil in a large skillet over medium-high heat. Sauté mushrooms and chicken until golden brown. Sprinkle with salt, tarragon, pepper, and parsley. Pour wine over chicken. Cover and simmer for 25 to 30 minutes. Remove chicken to serving platter. Deglaze skillet with a little water; thicken with one teaspoon arrowroot, if desired. Serve sauce with chicken and prepared vermicelli.

Brussels Sprouts and Creamed Carrots

Makes 4 servings

1 pound Brussels sprouts
   Salt and freshly ground pepper

Creamed Carrots

Trim off sprout ends and cut an "X" in the stem of each. Add sprouts to boiling water. Reduce heat; simmer, uncovered, until tender, 10 to 15 minutes. Drain; transfer to a serving platter and season with salt and ground pepper. Fit a pastry bag with a fluted tip. Pipe a rosette of Creamed Carrots on each Brussels sprout. Pipe remaining Creamed Carrots around edge of platter.

Creamed Carrots

Makes 4 servings

3 carrots, sliced diagonally
4 ounces Neufchatel cheese
2 tablespoons plain yogurt

¼ teaspoon tarragon
   Skim milk

Steam carrots until tender, 5 to 8 minutes. Combine with remaining ingredients and purée until smooth. Thin with milk, if necessary. Serve with Brussels sprouts as directed.

Basil Shrimp and Zucchini
Beef Tenderloin with
Mushrooms and Bordeaux Sauce
Baked Potato Slices
Cream of Green Bean and Parsnip Soup

A good saucier can always whip up a brown sauce, fast and fresh. Here is a basic Bordeaux sauce for beef that is also superb over game and chops.

Basil Shrimp and Zucchini
Makes 4 servings

1 medium zucchini
1 medium crookneck squash
¼ cup basil mustard
½ cup Neufchatel *or* cream cheese
¼ cup plain yogurt

1 to 2 tablespoons minced fresh basil
1 teaspoon sherry vinegar
1 pound cooked baby shrimp
Chopped fresh basil

Shred zucchini and squash. Sauté in medium skillet until heated through, about 5 minutes. In a bowl, mix next 5 ingredients. Fold in shrimp. Spread squash mixture on a plate. Mound shrimp mixture on top. Garnish with basil.

Beef Tenderloin with Mushrooms and Bordeaux Sauce
Makes 4 servings

1 tablespoon butter
1 tablespoon oil
1½ pounds tenderloin steak, sliced
 ¾ inch thick, cut into 4 equal pieces

¼ pound sliced mushrooms
Bordeaux Sauce

Heat butter and oil in a wide frying pan over medium-high heat. Brown steak well on both sides, 3 to 5 minutes per side for rare meat. Sauté mushrooms in meat juices and keep warm. At serving time, spoon mushrooms and Bordeaux Sauce over each steak and pass the rest separately.

Bordeaux Sauce

Makes 2 cups

1 tablespoon butter
2 cloves garlic, minced
½ medium onion, diced
½ medium carrot, diced
1¼ cups rich beef stock
4 sprigs parsley
1 bay leaf

¼ teaspoon thyme leaves
¼ teaspoon basil leaves
1 tablespoon arrowroot
½ cup fine Bordeaux wine
Freshly ground pepper
Minced fresh parsley

Melt butter in medium saucepan; sauté garlic, onion, and carrots until well browned, about 8 minutes. Mix in next 5 ingredients. Bring to a boil, reduce heat and simmer 15 to 20 minutes. Strain. Return to pan and reduce to 1 cup over high heat. Combine arrowroot and wine; whisk into pan. Simmer until thickened, whisking constantly, about 1 minute. Sprinkle with pepper and parsley.

Baked Potato Slices

Makes 4 servings

Vegetable oil
4 large Russet potatoes
Salt

Freshly ground pepper
Chopped chives, optional
Butter, optional

Preheat oven to 400°. Grease cookie sheet with oil. Scrub potatoes and cut into ⅛-inch slices. Spread potatoes on cookie sheet and season to taste with salt and pepper. Bake about 10 minutes, then turn slices and continue baking, another 10 minutes, or until browned and tender. Serve garnished with chives and butter, if desired.

Cream of Green Bean and Parsnip Soup

Makes 4 servings

1 large parsnip, thinly sliced
¼ cup white rice
2 quarts water
1 pound green beans, cut to 1-inch lengths
2 tablespoons unsalted butter

½ teaspoon salt
¼ cup dry sherry
2 cups milk
Freshly ground pepper
Freshly ground nutmeg

Prepare 2 days in advance, then refrigerate. Place parsnip and rice in a 3-quart saucepan; add water and bring to a boil. Reduce heat, cover, and simmer 10 minutes. Add green beans and simmer until beans are soft, 10 to 15 minutes. Drain well, reserving liquid. Process or purée bean mixture, adding remaining ingredients and reserved liquid, as needed. Reheat purée on low heat. Add pepper and nutmeg to taste.

Beef Tenderloin with Mushrooms and Bordeaux Sauce, page 93; Braised Celery and Red Peppers, page 57; Baked Potato Slices, this page.

Creamy Herbal Walnut Soup
Orange Piquant Fish
Avocado Rice
Baked Mushrooms
Baked Squash Slices
Red and Green Side Salad

Creamy Herbal Walnut Soup has a quiet color and a unique flavor. Appropriately, it serves as a subtle backdrop for the snappy Orange Piquant Fish and the vibrant colors of the accompanying dishes.

Creamy Herbal Walnut Soup
Makes 4 servings

1½ cups chopped walnuts
2 cups lowfat milk
1 bay leaf
¼ teaspoon dried thyme
¼ teaspoon dried basil
2 tablespoons chopped parsley
1 tablespoon butter

1 medium onion, sliced
½ cup thinly sliced celery
2 tablespoons flour
3 cups chicken broth
2 tablespoons dry sherry
Salt and pepper to taste
Finely chopped chives *or* green onion

Cover walnuts with water in a saucepan. Boil 3 minutes; drain. In the same saucepan, pour milk over walnuts; add bay leaf, thyme, basil, and parsley. Scald, cover, and set aside 20 minutes. Melt butter in a 3-quart saucepan; add onion and celery. Sauté 5 minutes. Blend in flour and cook until bubbly. Gradually stir in the broth; cook, stirring continuously, until soup boils. Reduce heat and simmer gently for 20 minutes. Remove bay leaf; add milk and walnut mixture. Purée in blender. (At this point, purée can be covered and refrigerated until serving time.) Just before serving, reheat to simmering. Add sherry, salt, and pepper to taste. Sprinkle individual servings with chives.

Baked Squash Slices
Makes 4 servings

1 small acorn squash
1 large zucchini squash

Olive oil *or* vegetable oil
Salt and freshly ground pepper

Peel and cut squashes into ¼-inch slices. Arrange in shallow baking dish. Drizzle oil over squash and season to taste. Cover and bake in 450° oven until tender, 15 to 20 minutes.

Orange Piquant Fish
Makes 4 servings

1½ pounds fresh fish fillets
1 tablespoon butter
¼ cup minced red onion
2 cloves garlic, minced
⅓ cup minced parsley
1 cup orange juice

¼ cup chopped olives
3 jalapeno chilies, chopped
1 cup orange juice
Avocado slices
Watercress sprigs

Arrange fillets in a baking dish. Melt butter in saucepan; sauté onion and garlic until soft. Add parsley and stir in orange juice. Spread olives and chilies on top of fish; pour sauce evenly over all. Bake at 450° for 10 to 15 minutes. Garnish with avocado slices and watercress sprigs.

Baked Mushrooms
Makes 4 servings

¾ pound (30 medium) mushrooms
2 to 3 tablespoons dry sherry
¼ cup minced fresh parsley

Salt and freshly ground pepper to taste
Sour cream

Arrange mushrooms on a large piece of foil. Sprinkle with sherry, parsley, salt, and pepper. Seal foil tightly around mushrooms. Bake in 450° oven for 20 minutes. Top individual servings with sour cream, or combine mushrooms and sour cream in a large serving dish.

Red and Green Side Salad
Makes 4 servings

1 cucumber, sliced
1 small red onion, separated into rings
10 to 12 cherry tomatoes, halved

Flavored wine vinegar
Walnut oil or vegetable oil
Minced herbs, optional

Layer cucumbers and red onion around 4 salad plates. Place tomatoes in center. Combine vinegar and oil to taste; sprinkle over vegetables. Garnish with herbs, if desired, and serve at room temperature.

Avocado Rice
Makes 4 servings

1 cup wild rice or long-grain rice
¼ teaspoon salt
1 cup white wine or water

1 cup chicken broth
½ cup diced avocado or jicama
¼ cup minced cilantro or parsley

Combine rice, salt, wine, and broth in a saucepan; bring to a boil. Reduce heat, cover and simmer until liquid is absorbed, 20 minutes. Just before serving, toss with avocado and cilantro.

Savory Parmesan Wheels
Broiled Salmon and Linguine with
Watercress Sauce
Minted Carrots
Sliced Beefsteak Tomatoes

*Savory Parmesan Wheels are a delightful introduction to this
menu laced with the delicate flavor and fragrance of
watercress. Carrots, with a hint of mint, are the perfect accent.*

Sliced Beefsteak Tomatoes
Makes 4 servings

3 large beefsteak tomatoes
⅓ cup olive oil *or* vegetable oil
¼ cup lemon juice
1 tablespoon chopped fresh basil *or*
　½ teaspoon dried basil

1 tablespoon fresh chopped rosemary *or*
　½ teaspoon dried rosemary

Slice tomatoes. Whisk together remaining ingredients; pour over tomatoes. Let stand at room temperature until serving.

Broiled Salmon and Linguine
with Watercress Sauce
Makes 4 servings

4 salmon steaks, ¾ inch thick
1 tablespoon chopped fresh marjoram *or*
　1 teaspoon dried marjoram
Salt and pepper to taste

Watercress Sauce
4 ounces thin linguine, cooked and
　well-drained

Sprinkle both sides of fish with marjoram and salt and pepper to taste. On an oiled rack 4 inches from heat source, broil steaks until first side is lightly browned, 5 to 8 minutes. Turn and broil 5 to 8 minutes more, until fish flakes easily when tested with a fork. Combine ¾ cup of Watercress Sauce with prepared linguine. Serve balance of the Watercress Sauce over the salmon steaks.

Watercress Sauce

Makes 2 cups

1 cup tightly packed parsley
1 cup watercress leaves
6 large Boston lettuce leaves, centers removed
3 large shallots, quartered

1 small onion, cut into 1-inch chunks
3 tablespoons olive oil *or* vegetable oil
1 tablespoon wine vinegar
⅓ cup unsalted tomato juice

Fit food processor with steel blade. Combine parsley, watercress, lettuce, shallots, and onions in work bowl; process with 3 on/off turns. Scrape down side of bowl. Pour olive oil over mixture in a circular motion. Sprinkle with vinegar. Purée for 5 seconds. While machine is running, pour tomato juice through feed tube until well blended. Serve with salmon and linguine as directed.

Savory Parmesan Wheels

Makes 4 servings

1 cup butter
1 cup flour
½ cup shredded sharp Muenster *or* sharp Brick cheese
½ cup sour cream
⅔ cup freshly grated Parmesan *or* Romano cheese

½ teaspoon cayenne pepper
½ teaspoon paprika
¼ teaspoon salt
¼ teaspoon Tabasco sauce
    Fresh cut vegetables or fruit, optional

Using a pastry blender, cut together butter and flour. Blend in Muenster and sour cream. Divide dough into 4 parts; wrap and chill for 15 minutes. Combine Parmesan, pepper, paprika, salt, and Tabasco sauce; set aside. On a floured surface, roll one part of pastry into a 12 x 6-inch rectangle. Sprinkle with 2 tablespoons of the Parmesan mixture. Fold in 6-inch sides to meet in center, forming a square. Sprinkle with 1 tablespoon of the Parmesan mixture. Fold in open ends to meet in center. Fold in half lengthwise; flatten lightly. Fold lengthwise again. On folded edge, make ¼-inch cuts, 1 inch apart. Bring ends together, forming a wheel, and place on ungreased baking sheet. Repeat with remaining pastry sections. Bake 10 to 15 minutes at 450° or until golden brown. Serve with vegetables or fruit, if desired.

Minted Carrots

Makes 4 servings

1 tablespoon butter
3 cups thinly sliced carrots
¼ cup water

2 tablespoons chopped fresh mint, *or*
2 teaspoons dried mint
Salt and freshly ground pepper to taste

In a large frying pan, melt butter over high heat. Add carrots and water. Cover and cook until liquid evaporates, 5 to 8 minutes. Stir occasionally. Stir in mint and season with salt and pepper to taste.

Overleaf: Broiled Salmon and Linguine with Watercress Sauce, Sliced Beefsteak Tomatoes, page 98; Minted Carrots, this page.

> **Avocado Kebabs with Tangy Mustard Dip**
> **Oven-Fried Fish Fillets**
> **Potato Latkes**
> **Carrots Vichy**
> **Tomato Aux Gratin**
> **Country Greens Soup**

*The cool color and flavor of avocados are an attractive
introduction to this light menu. Crispy Potato Latkes are a
refreshing complement to golden Oven-Fried Fish Fillets.
The soup is another fresh and fragrant
accompaniment to fish.*

Avocado Kebabs with Tangy Mustard Dip

Makes 4 servings

2 avocados, seeded, peeled, and cubed
  Lemon juice as needed
4 ounces Cheddar cheese, cubed
4 ounces salami, cubed
4 ounces Swiss *or* Monterey Jack
  cheese, cubed

4 cherry tomatoes *or* ripe olives
  Red *or* green apple slices
  Tangy Mustard Dip

Dip avocado cubes in lemon juice. Immediately assemble all ingredients, except
Tangy Mustard Dip, on 6-inch skewers, according to ingredient list. Lay skewers across
apple slices and serve with Tangy Mustard Dip.

Tangy Mustard Dip

Makes 1 cup

½ cup plain yogurt
½ cup cottage cheese

2 tablespoons Dijon-style mustard
⅛ teaspoon garlic powder

Process or blend all ingredients until smooth. Chill at least 15 minutes before serving.

Oven-Fried Fish Fillets

Makes 4 servings

1 pound boneless fish fillets *or* small
  whole fish
¼ cup Vinaigrette (page 65)

1 cup dry bread crumbs
Lemon wedges
Minced parsley

Preheat oven to 500°. Dip fish into Vinaigrette, then into bread crumbs. Arrange on an oiled baking pan or an oven-proof platter. Drizzle any remaining Vinaigrette over fish. Bake for 10 to 12 minutes, or until the fish flakes easily when tested with a fork. Garnish with lemon and parsley.

Potato Latkes

Makes 4 servings

2 medium baking potatoes, grated
2 medium yellow crookneck squash,
  shredded
¼ cup minced parsley
¼ cup minced green onion
⅓ cup grated Romano *or* Parmesan
  cheese, optional

1 to 2 tablespoons butter
1 to 2 tablespoons safflower oil *or*
  vegetable oil
Sour cream *or* plain yogurt, optional

Wrap grated potatoes in a cheesecloth; press to absorb moisture. Combine squash, parsley, onion, and cheese, if desired; blend well. Melt butter in a large sauté pan; add oil. Drop heaping spoonfuls of batter into pan. Press into 4-inch patties about ¼ inch thick. Fry until crisp and brown on both sides. Serve very hot with sour cream. *Note:* To keep latkes warm, place on a baking sheet lined with paper towels and place in a 200° oven.

Tomato Aux Gratin

Makes 4 servings

2 beefsteak tomatoes, halved
2 tablespoons melted butter
½ cup bread *or* cracker crumbs
2 tablespoons dry white wine *or* chicken
  broth

½ teaspoon basil
½ teaspoon thyme
½ teaspoon paprika

Gently remove seeds from tomato halves. Combine remaining ingredients and divide evenly among tomato halves, pressing lightly into each. Broil on oiled foil for 10 minutes.

Country Greens Soup

Makes 4 servings

1 teaspoon butter
1 bunch green onions, thinly sliced
1 large red onion, sliced
1 cup chopped celery
1 cup shredded carrots
2 cans (14 ounces each) low-sodium chicken broth *or* 3½ cups rich broth
3 zucchini *or* crookneck squash, thinly sliced

1 bunch Swiss chard *or* coarsely chopped spinach *or* 1 package (10 ounces) frozen chopped chard *or* broccoli, thawed
½ teaspoon marjoram
Salt, pepper, and lemon juice to taste

Melt butter in a 3-quart saucepan. Stir in green onions, red onion, celery, and carrots. Cook, covered, until celery begins to soften, about 10 minutes. Add broth; bring to simmer. Simmer greens for 2 minutes. Add zucchini; simmer 3 minutes. Add Swiss chard; simmer 5 minutes. Add marjoram; season to taste with salt, pepper, and lemon juice.

Carrots Vichy

Makes 4 servings

1 pound baby carrots, trimmed
Boiling salted water
2 tablespoons butter

2 tablespoons Cognac *or* lemon juice
1 tablespoon honey *or* brown sugar

Place carrots in a large sauté pan. Cover with salted water and simmer, covered, until tender-crisp, 8 to 10 minutes. Drain. Push carrots to one side and stir in remaining ingredients. Sauté carrots, shaking pan, over medium-high heat.

Variations

◆ **Orange:** Omit Cognac and honey. Add ½ to 1 teaspoon minced ginger and 1 to 2 tablespoons orange juice concentrate. Sprinkle with grated orange rind, if desired.

◆ **Creamy Onion:** Add 2 to 3 sliced scallions to sauté pan during last 4 to 5 minutes of carrot cooking time. Just before serving, stir in ⅓ cup yogurt, ⅓ cup cream cheese, and ¼ teaspoon freshly ground pepper.

> **Crudités with Garlic Dip**
> **Champagned Fish with**
> **Maitre D'Hotel Butter**
> **Toasted Baguettes**
> **Steamed Vegetable Mélange**
> **Chilled Fruit Soup**

This elegant entrée is particularly good for dry fish fillets, as they benefit from the moistening and flavor of the champagne. The Maitre D'Hotel Butter is easy and excellent with both fish and baguettes; and your guests will be charmed by the sunny, make-ahead Chilled Fruit Soup.

Steamed Vegetable Mélange
Makes 4 servings

2 medium carrots, thinly sliced
¼ cup green beans, cut into thirds
1 cup cauliflower florets

1 tablespoon fresh lemon juice
1 teaspoon grated lemon peel

Steam vegetables over boiling water until tender-crisp, about 8 minutes. Toss in a serving bowl with lemon juice and peel.

Chilled Fruit Soup
Makes 4 servings

5 large ripe bananas *or* nectarines, peeled and quartered *or* 1 bag frozen peaches *or* nectarines, thawed
1 tablespoon fructose
½ cup Neufchatel cheese
¼ cup plain yogurt
2 tablespoons orange juice concentrate, thawed

1 tablespoon lemon juice
2 to 3 tablespoons sweet *or* cream sherry
Kiwi fruit slices
Fresh mint sprigs

In a blender or food processor, blend all ingredients, except kiwi and mint, until smooth. Taste and add additional lemon or sherry as desired. Pour into a serving bowl; cover and chill. Garnish with kiwi fruit slices and fresh mint sprigs.

Crudités with Garlic Dip

Makes 4 servings

4 medium cloves garlic
2 large egg yolks, at room temperature
⅛ teaspoon salt
¼ teaspoon Dijon-style mustard
¾ cup olive oil *or* vegetable oil
1 teaspoon lemon juice
½ teaspoon cold water

1 cup cauliflower florets, steamed
1 cup broccoli florets, steamed
4 green onions, trimmed
½ cup fresh mushrooms
4 carrots, cut into 3-inch sticks
4 stalks celery, cut into 3-inch sticks

Crush garlic and reduce it to a paste; place in a blender or food processor. Add egg yolks, salt, and mustard; blend briefly. Gradually stir in half the oil. Add lemon and water; add the remaining oil; blend slowly and steadily. Transfer to a glass serving bowl; cover and refrigerate. To serve, place dip in the center of a large platter and arrange vegetables around it.

Champagned Fish with Maitre D'Hotel Butter

Makes 4 servings

Freshly ground pepper
4 1¼-pound fish steaks, cut 1 inch thick
(halibut, swordfish, snapper,
or salmon)

½ cup champagne
Maitre D'Hotel Butter

Grind pepper generously over steaks. Pour champagne evenly over fish. Broil 4 inches from heat source for 3 to 5 minutes. Turn. Broil 4 minutes more or until fish flakes easily when tested with a fork. Top with a spoonful of Maitre D'Hotel Butter.

Maitre D'Hotel Butter

Makes ¾ cup

½ cup butter, at room temperature
¼ cup grated Parmesan cheese

½ cup chopped fresh parsley
1 to 2 cloves garlic, minced

Combine all ingredients; blend well. Serve as directed.

Toasted Baguettes

Makes 4 servings

4 fresh baguettes

¼ cup Maitre D'Hotel Butter

Slice baguettes and spread evenly with Maitre D'Hotel Butter. Broil 4 inches from heat source until golden brown.

Chilled Fruit Soup, Steamed Vegetable Mélange,
page 105; Champagned Fish with Maitre D'Hotel
Butter, Toasted Baguettes, this page.
***Overleaf:** Burrito Buffet, page 110; Great Guacamole,*
Mexican Salad, Super Nachos Supreme, page 111;
Elote Mexican Corn, page 112.

Super Nachos Supreme with
Great Guacamole
Burrito Buffet
Mexican Salad with Poppy
Seed Dressing
Elote Mexican Corn

*Invite your guests to assemble their own burritos from a
grandé assortment of meats, fresh vegetables, and garnishes.
Do all the cooking ahead — enjoy your own party!*

Burrito Buffet

Makes 12 burritos or 4 servings

1 pound beef top round *or* sirloin
1 pound chicken breasts, skinned and boned *or* turkey tenderloins
½ teaspoon ground cumin
½ teaspoon coarsely chopped chilies *or* crushed red pepper
2 to 3 cloves garlic, minced
2 teaspoons butter
2 teaspoons safflower oil
4 to 6 ounces low-fat Farmers cheese, shredded

1 large onion, thinly sliced
4 to 6 radishes, trimmed and thinly sliced
1 cup salsa
12 flour tortillas
Assorted garnishes such as: avocados, olives, cilantro sprigs, green onions, green chilies, and plain yogurt

Slice chicken into ½-inch wide strips. Slice steak on the diagonal into ⅜-inch thick pieces, then into strips. Sprinkle chicken and steak evenly with cumin, chopped chilies, and garlic; rub in lightly with fingertips. Heat a non-stick sauté pan over high heat. Add 1 teaspoon butter and 1 teaspoon oil. Add about half of the chicken strips. Sauté until browned on both sides, about 2 minutes. Transfer to a serving dish; cover to keep warm. Repeat with remaining chicken. Heat remaining butter and oil; sauté steak, about half at a time, until browned. Place in the serving dish alongside the chicken with bowls of cheese, onion, radishes, and salsa. Warm tortillas in the oven, then transfer to a towel-lined basket. Serve with a selection of garnishes.

Super Nachos Supreme with Great Guacamole

Makes 4 servings

4 cups tortilla chips
1 cup canned refried beans, plain
   or spicy
1 cup taco sauce
1 cup shredded Monterey Jack cheese
1 cup shredded Cheddar cheese
¼ cup sliced olives
1 tomato, diced

2 to 3 tablespoons minced green onion
Great Guacamole
Sour cream
Taco sauce
Cilantro sprigs
Sliced radishes
Diced green chilies

Arrange chips on a large platter. Cover evenly with beans, sauce, and cheese. Microwave or broil 1 minute, until cheese is melted. Top with olives, tomato, and onion. Serve with Great Guacamole and remaining ingredients; let guests garnish their own serving portions.

Great Guacamole

Makes 4 servings

2 ripe avocados, mashed
2 tablespoons plain yogurt
2 tablespoons lemon juice

½ cup taco sauce
1 small tomato, diced

In a small bowl, blend all ingredients to desired consistency, except tomato. Fold in tomato.

Mexican Salad

Makes 4 generous servings

½ medium head iceberg lettuce,
   shredded
½ bunch romaine, shredded
4 medium beets, fresh-cooked *or* canned,
   thinly sliced
4 oranges, peeled and thinly sliced
3 bananas, thinly sliced
2 grapefruit, peeled and thinly sliced
2 red apples, unpeeled and thinly sliced

2 green apples, unpeeled and thinly
   sliced
1 pineapple, peeled, cored, and thinly
   sliced
3 limes, peeled and thinly sliced
Seeds of 2 pomegranates
½ cup unsalted peanuts
Poppy Seed Dressing *or* Mexican
Dressing (page 112)

Place iceberg lettuce and romaine in a large, shallow glass bowl. Arrange beets and fruit attractively over lettuce. Sprinkle pomegranate seeds and nuts over all. Just before serving, pour dressing over salad; toss.

Poppy Seed Dressing

Makes 1½ cups

1 cup ricotta cheese
1 cup plain low-fat yogurt *or*
   walnut oil
1 to 3 tablespoons honey
Grated peel of 1 lemon

Grated peel of 1 lime
1 tablespoon lemon juice
1 tablespoon lime juice
2 to 3 tablespoons poppy seeds

In a blender or food processor, combine all ingredients. Blend until thoroughly combined.

Elote Mexican Corn

Makes 4 servings

3 ears of corn, in kernels *or*
   1 package (10 ounces) frozen corn
2 to 3 tablespoons water
1 clove garlic, minced

1 can (4 ounces) diced green chilies
2 to 3 tablespoons mild *or* hot sauce
1 tomato, diced

Cook corn and a little water in a covered saucepan over medium heat, about 5 minutes. Add remaining ingredients; increase heat and cook until heated through and tender, 5 to 10 minutes.

Variations

◆ **Tofu Corn**: Drain one 14½-ounce package tofu and freeze for 48 hours. Thaw and wrap tightly in cheesecloth, pressing to squeeze out liquid. Crumble and sprinkle over corn. Bake as directed or until cheese is melted.

◆ **Cheddar Corn**: Sprinkle ½ to 1 cup shredded Cheddar cheese over corn. Bake as directed.

Mushroom Cream Cheese Turnovers
Seafood Brochettes
Red Onion Rice
Steamed Medley of Vegetables with
Lemon Cream Sauce

*Here is an adventure in dining. Seafood Brochettes open the
door for exciting experimentation — try to incorporate some
of your favorite fish, fruit, and vegetable combinations
in addition to those suggested in the recipe.*

Mushroom Cream Cheese Turnovers

Makes 4 servings

1 package (8 ounces) Neufchatel *or*
   cream cheese, softened
½ cup butter, softened
1½ cups flour
1 tablespoon butter
1 red onion, finely chopped
2 shallots, minced
½ pound mushrooms *or* spinach,
   finely chopped

¼ teaspoon basil leaves
¼ teaspoon thyme leaves
¼ teaspoon salt
   Freshly ground black pepper to taste
2 tablespoons flour
½ cup sour cream

Blend cheese and ½ cup butter thoroughly with a wooden spoon. Add flour and work through with fingers until smooth. Freeze 10 minutes. Roll dough into ⅛-inch thickness on a lightly floured surface; cut into rounds using a 3-inch biscuit cutter.

To prepare filling, melt 1 tablespoon butter in a large skillet. Sauté onion and shallots until lightly browned. Add mushrooms, raise heat and cook, stirring continuously, until liquid is mostly evaporated. Add basil, thyme, salt, pepper, and flour; stir well. Stir in sour cream and cook over medium heat, until thickened.

Place a teaspoon of filling on each dough round and fold. Crimp edges with a fork. Prick top of crusts. Bake on ungreased baking sheet at 450° for 15 minutes, or until lightly browned. Serve hot.

Seafood Brochettes

Makes 4 servings

¼ pound large scallops
8 cherry tomatoes
¼ pound swordfish *or* sea bass, cut in
1-inch cubes
1 small green bell pepper, cut in small
squares

1 small onion, cut in 4 wedges
¼ pound halibut, cut in 1-inch cubes
Herbed Lemon Marinade *or*
Teriyaki Marinade
Lemon wedges

Alternately thread scallops, tomatoes, swordfish, green pepper, onion, and halibut on 4 metal skewers. Arrange in a shallow baking dish. Marinate each kabob, with choice of marinade, for at least 15 minutes. Broil 4 inches from heat source, about 4 minutes per side, basting often. Arrange on serving platter and garnish with lemon wedges.

Herbed Lemon Marinade

Makes 1½ cups

¾ cup safflower oil *or* vegetable oil
½ cup lemon juice
1 bay leaf

1 teaspoon chopped fresh basil
1 teaspoon chopped fresh thyme
1 teaspoon chopped fresh chives

Combine ingredients; blend well.

Teriyaki Marinade

Makes ¾ cup

½ cup soy sauce
2 tablespoons sugar
2 teaspoons grated fresh ginger

2 cloves garlic, minced
3 tablespoons dry sherry

In a bowl or tightly covered jar, combine ingredients. Mix or shake well until sugar is dissolved.

Red Onion Rice

Makes 4 servings

1 package (6 ounces) wild and
white rice
⅓ cup chopped red onion

¼ cup minced green onion *or* parsley
⅓ cup hazelnuts, almonds, *or* pine nuts,
chopped

Prepare rice according to package directions. Stir in red onion. Toss with green onion and nuts just before serving.

Steamed Medley of Vegetables with Lemon Cream
Sauce, page 116; Seafood Brochettes,
Red Onion Rice, this page.

Steamed Medley of Vegetables with Lemon Cream Sauce

Makes 4 servings

1 artichoke, cooked
  Lemon Cream Sauce
6 to 8 fresh mushrooms, halved
1 cup broccoli florets

1 cup cauliflower florets
4 baby carrots
3 baby turnips, halved
1 red pepper, cut into chunks

Hollow out center of artichoke and fill with Lemon Cream Sauce. Set aside. Arrange vegetables in a bamboo steamer, leaving a place in the center to place the artichoke after the vegetables are cooked. Steam, covered, for 8 to 10 minutes. In last few moments add artichoke to center. Serve in bamboo steamer.

Lemon Cream Sauce

Makes 1 cup

1 package (8 ounces) Neufchatel *or*
  cream cheese
2 tablespoons plain yogurt

2 tablespoons lemon juice
⅛ teaspoon turmeric *or* saffron
¼ cup milk

Combine all ingredients in a small saucepan. Cook over low heat, stirring often, until slightly thickened.

Dijon Sauce Variation

Makes 1 cup

2 egg yolks
1 tablespoon Dijon-style mustard
2 teaspoons white wine vinegar

½ cup vegetable oil
½ cup cream cheese
Salt and freshly ground pepper

Combine egg yolks and mustard in a blender or food processor. With motor running, slowly add vinegar in drops. Drizzle in oil, slowly increasing flow to a slow, steady stream. Blend in cheese. Season with salt and pepper to taste.

Egg Enchiladas
Papaya and Orange Smoothie

This brunch is easy to concoct for a crowd. The enchiladas can be made ahead and kept in the oven for up to an hour. Fruit shakes are not only fast, but nutritional also — this Papaya and Orange Smoothie is an authentic Mexican variation.

Egg Enchiladas
Makes 4 servings

2 teaspoons safflower oil
1 small red onion, chopped
½ green pepper, seeded and diced
2 jars (12 ounces each) salsa
8 to 10 eggs
¼ cup sliced jalapeno peppers

1 tablespoon butter
4 large corn tortillas
4 ounces medium Cheddar cheese
Sliced green onion
Sliced radishes
Chopped fresh cilantro *or* parsley

Heat oil in medium saucepan. Sauté onion and green pepper in oil. Add salsa and simmer, uncovered, about 10 minutes. Remove sauce from heat. In a bowl, mix eggs and jalapenos. In a large skillet over medium heat, melt butter. Scramble egg mixture in butter until eggs are cooked through, but still moist.

Dip tortillas in salsa mixture until soft. Spoon ¼ of the scrambled eggs down center of each tortilla; roll up, and place enchilada, seam side down, in a casserole dish. Repeat with each tortilla. Reheat remaining sauce to boiling. Pour evenly over enchiladas and sprinkle with cheese. Place under broiler, 4 inches from heat source, until cheese melts. Garnish with onion, radishes, and cilantro.

Papaya and Orange Smoothie
Makes 4 servings

1 ripe papaya, peeled, seeded, and chopped
2 cups orange juice
1 cup plain yogurt

1 cup cracked ice
1 banana, roughly chopped
1 teaspoon lime *or* lemon juice

Purée or process all ingredients until smooth. Serve in tall glasses.

DESSERTS

Desserts, too, can be fast and fresh. Keep the rest of the menu in mind as you plan the dessert. If the meal is hearty, serve a light sweet such as Hot Fruit Compote. A heartier dessert such as Hazelnut Meringues with Chocolate Mousse and a garnish of Chocolate Caraque is a choice conclusion for a light meal.

Desserts can also balance a menu nutritionally. If the main dish is primarily vegetarian, follow it with a dessert of eggs, cheese, milk, or yogurt. A superb option here would be Ambrosia Cheesecake, Cold Soufflé Cordon Bleu, or Chocolate Pots-de-Creme. If rice, potatoes, or pasta was not on the evening bill of fare, serve a dessert featuring bread, rice, or cake as the sweet flourish. Flaming Fig Sauce over pound cake would be a fast selection, or serve Fresh Ginger Cookies and Linzer Cream Wedges with richly brewed coffee.

No fruit in the menu? Include it in the dessert. Layer fresh chopped fruit in champagne flutes or parfait glasses, with a mixture of Neufchatel cream cheese and plain yogurt, lightly sweetened with honey. Variations on parfaits include toppings of chopped nuts, granola, liqueurs, and chopped candied fruit with mint sprigs. Try the Layered Applesauce Parfaits; they are also a delightful addition to any brunch.

A final word on fruit. Frozen berries are an acceptable substitution for fresh. They are available throughout the year and at relatively inexpensive prices. They produce excellent results in these recipes; when blended, their texture is often thicker than the fresh, and the flavor is more concentrated.

Consider preparation time and method as you select your dessert. Choose something that can be made at a convenient time for you — either a make-ahead recipe, or one that you can prepare along with the rest of the meal. This chapter offers a medley of options in each category. The Fresh Fruit Gelati will store for 2 to 3 months in your refrigerator. The Peach Fluff can be made 2 to 3 days in advance. Crepes and cold soufflés may be made ahead, as well, and refrigerated. If an entrée is prepared in the oven, bake a meringue alongside; Vacharin Fruit Tortes are elegant meringues, made with ease. Simply combine your level of energy and your imagination when planning desserts into your menu.

These desserts are designed to complement your new menus, but don't hesitate to try an unusual ingredient or garnish — make the recipe your own. Guests will be impressed with your exquisite finalés and you will enjoy the ease of entertaining, fast and fresh.

Fresh Fruit Gelati, page 120.

Fresh Fruit Gelati

Makes 1 quart

2 ripe bananas
2 ripe papayas
1 tablespoon orange juice
1 tablespoon lemon juice
1 tablespoon lime juice
1 tablespoon grated orange rind

1 tablespoon grated lemon rind
1 tablespoon grated lime rind
4 cups milk
½ cup sugar *or* ¼ cup fructose
1 teaspoon vanilla

Combine all ingredients in food processor. Process until blended. Transfer to shallow cake pan and freeze overnight. Process again, until smooth. Transfer to bowl and freeze overnight again. Scoop onto a puréed berry sauce or serve with cookies or fresh fruit slices.

Variations

◆ **Rhubarb-Strawberry**: Replace bananas and papayas with 2½ cups *each* sliced rhubarb and trimmed strawberries. Add additional sugar to taste.

◆ **Pineapple-Kiwi**: Replace bananas and papayas with 1 very ripe, peeled and chopped pineapple, plus 4 kiwi fruits, peeled and diced. Add a tablespoon of vodka, if desired.

Hot Fruit Compote

Makes 4 servings

½ cup dry white wine, champagne,
  or sparkling cider
1 tablespoon brown sugar, optional
¼ teaspoon ginger
¼ teaspoon nutmeg

¼ teaspoon cinnamon
½ thinly sliced lemon *or* lime
4 small peaches, apples, *or* 2 fresh
  pears, sliced

Combine all ingredients, except fruit, in a saucepan and bring to a boil. Reduce heat. Add fruit; cook and stir occasionally until tender, about 10 minutes. Serve warm.

Chocolate Pots-de-Creme

Makes 4 servings

2 cups whole milk *or* 1 cup *each*
  milk and half-and-half
6 ounces grated chocolate
6 egg yolks, lightly beaten

1 teaspoon vanilla *or* grated rind of
  1 orange *or* 1 tablespoon *each* instant
  coffee and Cognac

In a medium saucepan, stir milk and chocolate over medium heat until blended and scalded. Remove from heat; beat in eggs and vanilla. Strain and pour into four dainty serving cups. Chill.

Fruit Cobbler

Makes 4 servings

2 cans (16 ounces) sliced peaches, pears,
  or mixed fruit, reserve syrup
½ teaspoon ginger
½ teaspoon lemon juice
2 tablespoons cornstarch or tapioca
½ cup whole wheat flour
½ cup all-purpose flour

¼ teaspoon salt
½ teaspoon baking powder
2 tablespoons melted butter
¼ to ½ cup skim milk
¼ cup honey
  Oatmeal, to desired consistency

Thicken fruit syrup, ginger, and lemon juice with cornstarch or tapioca according to package directions. Gently fold in fruit; turn into a 9-inch baking dish. Combine remaining ingredients; roll out and place over fruit. Bake in a 450° oven, 10 to 15 minutes. Serve warm or at room temperature.

Peach Fluff

Makes 4 servings

¼ cup sugar
2 envelopes unflavored gelatin
¼ teaspoon salt
1 cup cold water
6 fresh peaches, diced or 1 package
  (20 ounces) frozen peach slices

1 to 2 tablespoons lemon juice
1 teaspoon almond extract
4 egg whites
1 package (2½ ounces) dessert
  topping mix
4 to 5 ladyfingers, split lengthwise

Combine first 3 ingredients in a saucepan. Add water; stir over medium heat until gelatin dissolves. Chill until partially set. Combine peaches, lemon juice, and almond extract. Combine gelatin, egg whites, and half of peaches in a large bowl. Beat with electric mixer until fluffy, about 10 minutes. Chill until partially set. Prepare dessert topping according to package directions. Fold remaining peaches and whipped topping into partially set gelatin. Line sides of 8-inch springform pan with lady fingers. Pour in filling. Chill until firm.

Linzer Cream Wedges

Makes 8 cookies

¼ cup butter, softened
¼ cup cream cheese, softened
¼ cup powdered sugar
¼ teaspoon vanilla or almond extract

1 cup flour
⅓ cup ground almonds or pecans
  or walnuts

Cream butter, cheese, and sugar. Fold in remaining ingredients. Roll out dough into a large circle about ¼ inch thick. Place on an ungreased baking sheet and cut into 8 wedges. Bake at 375° for 15 minutes or until golden brown. Serve warm with fruit or jam.

Cold Soufflé Cordon Bleu

Makes 4 servings

1 cup milk
½ vanilla pod, split, *or* 1 to 2 teaspoons
   vanilla extract
6 eggs, separated
½ to 1 cup sugar
1 envelope gelatin
¼ cup Cointreau, rum, *or* Grand Marnier
1 teaspoon grated orange rind

1 teaspoon grated lemon rind
1 cup whipping cream
2 tablespoons powdered sugar
6 to 8 shortbread cookies
   Additional Cointreau
   Mint leaves, fresh berries, citrus slices,
   or candied violets

Tie a band of greased foil around a soufflé dish; lightly oil a jam jar and place it in the center of the soufflé dish. Place a mixing bowl in the freezer. Scald milk with vanilla pod. Discard pod. Beat egg yolks with sugar until thick. Slowly pour hot milk into yolks, beating continually. Return to pan; cook over low heat until custard thickens and becomes creamy. Strain immediately, into the cold mixing bowl and return to freezer.

Soak and dissolve gelatin in liqueur over low heat. Add to custard with orange and lemon rind; mix thoroughly. Place in refrigerator until mixture is partially set. Beat egg whites until stiff. Beat cream and powdered sugar until stiff. Fold ½ of the whipped cream and all of the beaten egg whites into the custard. Pour quickly into soufflé dish around jam jar. Refrigerate until set.

Crush cookies and sprinkle with additional Cointreau. Gently twist jam jar and remove from the soufflé. Immediately, fill the cavity with crushed cookies. Decorate around outer edge with remaining whipped cream and garnish with mint leaves. Refrigerate. Remove foil just before serving.

Hint: A few ice cubes placed in the jam jar will help soufflé set faster.

Flaming Fig Sauce

Makes 4 servings

1 package (12 ounces) dried figs
1 to 1½ cups apple juice
2 teaspoons lemon juice
   Grated rind of 1 lemon
1 package (3½ ounces) whole almonds

¼ cup water
2 tablespoons cornstarch
3 to 4 tablespoons Cognac *or* brandy
4 slices of pound cake

Cover figs with apple juice in a medium saucepan. Bring to boiling point. Add lemon juice, lemon rind, and almonds. Reduce heat and simmer 20 minutes. Mix water and cornstarch; blend into fig sauce. Return to boil, stirring until thickened. Heat Cognac in small pan until simmering. Light and pour flaming Cognac into sauce. Spoon sauce over cake slices on individual serving plates.

*Dark Chocolate Fondue, Vacharin Fruit Torte,
page 125; Fresh Fruit Linzertorte, page 124;
Cold Soufflé Cordon Bleu, this page.*

Fresh Fruit Linzertorte

Makes one 9-inch torte

1 cup butter
⅓ cup sugar
2 egg yolks
1½ cups flour
1 cup ground almonds *or* hazelnuts
½ teaspoon cinnamon
½ teaspoon nutmeg
½ teaspoon ground ginger
Grated rind of 1 orange
Grated rind of 1 lemon
½ cup whipping cream
1 package (8 ounces) cream cheese, softened

1 tablespoon orange liqueur
Powdered sugar to taste
3 to 4 cups sliced fresh fruits of your choice (peaches, berries, plums, melons, apricots, apples)
½ cup orange marmalade, apricot preserves, red currant jelly, *or* raspberry jelly
2 tablespoons lemon juice
1 tablespoon orange liqueur

Cream butter and sugar. Beat in egg yolks. Mix in next 7 ingredients. Roll out dough and line a 9-inch tart or quiche pan. Place in refrigerator or freezer until thoroughly chilled. Bake 15 to 20 minutes at 375°; cool. Whip cream until it holds soft peaks. Beat in cream cheese, orange liqueur, and powdered sugar to taste. Spread on cooled crust in an even layer. Top with fruit in a desired pattern. In saucepan, heat preserves or marmalade; stir in juice and liqueur. Brush this glaze on fruit. Serve Linzertorte at room temperature.
Note: Use orange colored glaze ingredients for light fruit, red glaze for dark fruit.

Ambrosia Cheesecake

Makes one 12-inch cake

1 cup butter
¼ cup sugar
2 egg yolks
1½ cups flour
½ cup ground pecans, walnuts, hazelnuts, *or* almonds
¼ teaspoon *each* cinnamon, nutmeg, and allspice
8 ounces Neufchatel *or* cream cheese
½ pound fresh tofu, drained *or* additional cream cheese

½ cup plain yogurt
1 teaspoon vanilla
¼ to ½ cup honey
Grated rind of one orange
Grated rind of one lemon
½ cup ground nutmeats, optional
½ cup white *or* yellow raisins, optional
Orange halves
Lemon slices

Cream butter and sugar. Beat in yolks. Mix in flour, nuts, and spices. With your hands, shape dough into a smooth shiny ball. Press into 12-inch springform pan. Chill in freezer. Preheat oven to 400°. Bake crust until golden brown, 20 to 30 minutes. Cool. Combine all remaining ingredients, except orange halves and lemon slices; blend until smooth. Pour into pecan pie crust. Garnish with orange halves and lemon slices.

Vacharin Fruit Tortes

Makes 4 servings

5 egg whites
3 to 4 tablespoons powdered sugar *or* fructose
½ cup powdered cocoa *or* ground nuts
1 cup Creme Chantilly

2 cups raspberries, strawberries, *or* diced fruit of your choice
Powdered sugar

Preheat oven to 350°. Grease a baking sheet and dust with powdered sugar. Beat egg whites until they form soft peaks. Slowly add sugar until stiff peaks form. Fold in cocoa or nuts. Pipe or spoon mixture onto prepared baking sheet in 4 circles; with the back of a spoon, make small wells in the centers. Bake in oven until set, about 10 minutes. Cool. Fill with Creme Chantilly and berries. Dust with powdered sugar. Chill and serve.

Creme Chantilly

Makes 1 cup

½ cup whipping cream
½ cup cream cheese

Powdered sugar to taste
Cognac to taste

Whip together cream and cream cheese. Flavor with sugar and Cognac. Serve with Pear Pastries as directed.

Dark or White Chocolate Cream Fondue

Makes 4 servings

8 ounces semi-sweet dark chocolate, broken *or* sweet white chocolate
½ cup cream
3 to 5 teaspoons Cognac, liqueur, *or* expresso

Angel food cake, cubed
Fruit slices (oranges, strawberries, pineapple, bananas, dried fruits, kiwi, papaya)

Combine chocolate and cream in a heavy-bottomed saucepan. Cook over medium heat, stirring constantly, until the mixture is warm and most of the chocolate has melted. Remove from heat and stir in Cognac until chocolate is completely melted and smooth. Strain into a bowl. Let cool to room temperature. Thoroughly mix before using. Serve as a dip with angel food cake and fruit slices.
Note: Do not refrigerate. May be kept at room temperature, covered, for up to 2 days.

Fresh Ginger Cookies

Makes 3 dozen

¼ cup brown sugar
¼ cup unsalted butter
1 egg, lightly beaten
⅛ teaspoon vanilla extract
1 teaspoon fresh ginger
1 teaspoon minced candied ginger

½ teaspoon baking soda
¼ teaspoon allspice
¼ teaspoon cinnamon
¼ teaspoon cloves
¼ teaspoon ginger
1⅓ cups all-purpose flour

Preheat oven to 375°. Cream sugar and butter. Beat in egg and vanilla. Stir in spices and flour. Drop teaspoonfuls of batter onto a buttered and floured baking sheet 2 inches apart. Bake for 6 to 7 minutes.

Layered Fruits with Citrus-Honey Ricotta

Makes 4 servings

1 cup ricotta cheese
1 cup cream cheese
  Grated rind of 1 lemon
  Grated rind of 1 orange
  Grated rind of 1 lime
1 to 2 tablespoons lemon juice
1 to 2 tablespoons orange juice

1 to 2 tablespoons lime juice
¼ cup honey
2 to 3 tablespoons fresh chopped mint, optional
  Sliced fresh fruits (peaches, berries, bananas, plums)
  Fresh mint leaves, optional

Combine cheeses, fruit rind, fruit juices, honey, and chopped mint, if desired; blend well. Layer mixture with sliced fruit in parfait glasses. Chill before serving. Garnish with fresh mint sprigs.

Layered Applesauce Parfaits

Makes 4 servings

1 tablespoon butter
1 cup quick-cooking oats
1 tablespoon fructose
1 package (8 ounces) Neufchatel cheese
2 bananas, sliced *or* fruit of your choice
1 pinch coriander

1 jar (8 ounces) unsweetened applesauce
  Toasted chopped pecans, almonds, *or* walnuts
  Ground allspice, nutmeg, cinnamon, *or* coriander

Melt butter in saucepan over medium heat. Add oats and cook, stirring constantly, until oats are golden. Stir in fructose; remove from heat. Process or blend cheese, bananas, and coriander. Layer oats, cheese mixture, and applesauce in 4 large parfait glasses. Top layer should be cheese mixture. Sprinkle with nuts and spice. Serve at room temperature.

Hazelnut Meringues with Chocolate Mousse

Makes 4 servings

2 quarts water
½ teaspoon cream of tartar
5 egg whites
3 to 4 tablespoons powdered sugar

⅔ cup ground hazelnuts *or* almonds
Chocolate Mousse
Powdered chocolate

In a large, wide, frying pan, bring water and cream of tartar to a boil. Reduce heat. Beat egg whites until they form soft peaks. Slowly beat in sugar until stiff peaks form. Fold in ground nuts. Mound ¼ of the whites onto a perforated skimmer and smooth gently into a dome-shaped island. Gently place skimmer on the surface of the hot water until egg whites are released and float. Repeat for 3 more islands. Simmer 6 to 8 minutes or until egg whites are set. *Do not let islands float into each other.* Drain on a clean towel; cool. To serve, chill 4 glass plates. Spread Chocolate Mousse on chilled plates and center a Hazelnut Meringue on each. Garnish with a dusting of powdered chocolate. Chill until serving.

Chocolate Mousse

Makes 4 servings

8 ounces semi-sweet chocolate
1 cup semi-sweet butter
¼ to ⅓ cup sugar
6 eggs

3 to 4 tablespoons Hazelnut Liqueur, Armagnac, Kahlua, *or* concentrated expresso
Chocolate Caraque, optional

Melt chocolate in top of double boiler or in microwave oven. Beat butter and sugar with electric mixer at high speed until light and fluffy. Add melted chocolate and eggs, *one at a time,* beating well after each until thoroughly blended. Stir in liqueur. Serve with Hazelnut Meringues as directed.

Note: Once Chocolate Mousse has been spread over chilled plates, whipped cream may be streaked in for a ripple design. Chocolate Mousse is also delicious without Hazelnut Meringues; garnish with Chocolate Caraque, if desired.

Chocolate Caraque

Melt 3 ounces grated cooking chocolate on a plate over hot water and work with a palette knife until smooth. Spread thinly on a marble slab or laminated surface and leave until nearly set. Using a long, sharp knife, and working slantwise across the slab, shave the chocolate in long thin strokes. The chocolate should roll over itself, forming long scrolls.

INDEX